SHINE

SHINE

UNDERSTANDING ADHD SO YOUR CHILD CAN BE A STAR!

DR. BRANDI BOLLING

publish your gift

SHINE

Copyright © 2021 Brandi Bolling

All rights reserved.

Published by Publish Your Gift®
An imprint of Purposely Created Publishing Group, LLC

No part of this book may be reproduced, distributed or transmitted in any form by any means, graphic, electronic, or mechanical, including photocopy, recording, taping, or by any information storage or retrieval system, without permission in writing from the publisher, except in the case of reprints in the context of reviews, quotes, or references.

Printed in the United States of America

ISBN: 978-1-64484-379-6 (print)
ISBN: 978-1-64484-380-2 (ebook)

Special discounts are available on bulk quantity purchases by book clubs, associations and special interest groups. For details email: sales@publishyourgift.com or call (888) 949-6228.
For information logon to: www.PublishYourGift.com

DEDICATION

I dedicate this book to my family in its entirety. From the beginning of my professional career, you supported me with your time, thoughts, and money. As early as kindergarten, you rallied behind me when I performed, no matter how grand or small my role. In my adulthood, you taxied my children so that I could complete one goal after another. And since I have been a physician, you continue to spend countless hours telling others about my passion for helping families overcome challenges associated with ADHD. Too often, I know you prayed for me—for traveling grace, for me to pass an exam, or to survive the snow as I lived away from my native warm, southern city. And I will never forget the "tokens of love," which came with accompanying notes to "use it to get something to eat," I received in the mail from you.

To my husband, Frederic (Fred): God gave me the best friend, spouse, and father for our children when he allowed us to cross paths. You have been my biggest supporter, making it easy for me to reach my goals. While practicing law, you continue to move our family forward as I spend hours in my home office, creating works like this book and realizing many other dreams. I love you and appreciate you for everything.

To my mom, Diane Rudolph: thank you for showing me endless love and invaluable life lessons. You certainly are my biggest fan and the best babysitter in the world! I appreciate your belief in me and your you-can-do-it nudge and smile. You are my biggest role model. I am forever grateful for the sacrifices you and my daddy, Rodney Rudolph, made so this day could be possible.

Thank you to my children, Frederic, Franklin, and Faith. I love you beyond any words I can write. All of this I do for you.

Thank you, God. It is only through you that anything I have or hope to be or do is possible.

This book is in memory of my father, Rodney Rudolph, who met all my needs and wants, and whose smile made my day. I love and miss you.

TABLE OF CONTENTS

Acknowledgments 1

Foreword 3

Preface 5

Introduction 7

CHAPTER ONE:
Understanding ADHD 9

CHAPTER TWO:
Diagnosing ADHD 21

CHAPTER THREE:
The Changing Faces of ADHD:
Knowing How It Presents 47

CHAPTER FOUR:
Treating ADHD 55

CHAPTER FIVE:
Treating Comorbid Disorders of ADHD 111

CHAPTER SIX:
Advocating for Your Child with ADHD 125

CHAPTER SEVEN:
Moving Forward with ADHD 141

Thank You 145

Notes 147

About the Author 155

ACKNOWLEDGMENTS

Thank you to my husband, Attorney Frederic Bolling, my business coach, Dr. Draion Burch, and my mentor, Dr. Jacqueline Stewart, for each playing key roles in my beginning, forging ahead, and completing this book.

FOREWORD

As a general pediatrician for the past forty-three years, I've found that one of the areas that is still of questionable understanding is that of mental health. Although, in practice, we would rather refer all patients with mental health issues to those who are more focused in this area, it is often necessary that we address and treat our patients in our practices.

When I was president of our county chapter of the American Academy of Pediatrics (AAP), one of the projects of my tenure was a survey and comparison of the individual pediatric practices and how each one handled their patients with mental health issues, especially ADHD and ADD. We compared the methods of screening, including diagnostic criteria and treatment. Needless to say, there were almost as many methods and philosophies as there were respondents to the survey. It did open our eyes to the fact that as general practitioners, if we are to lighten the load on our mental health colleagues, we needed lots of help in the form of standardizing our approach to these patients. Because the mental health system is so overwhelmed it often takes prolonged wait times to get appointments. Insurance issues often present barriers. Consequently, there are "pseudo" clinics and situations that just hang out a shingle and pass out pills without the thorough evaluation and proper diagnosis, which is not only frustrating to us, but often inadequate or incorrect treatment for our patients. So, they end up back in our office with the same and additional problems as the ones we sent them out with in the first place.

ADD and ADHD have long been a nemesis in treating children. These diagnoses are on the minds of many parents (and sometimes teachers) for any child that may not be making straight As or who may have been sent to the principal's office for behavior. Or it may be the child who does not want to get up for school in the morning or the adolescent who defies their parents' rules.

To have a reference book that standardizes diagnosis and treatment is a reference that is long-awaited and absolutely necessary. This book will revolutionize the general office practice when it comes to the mental health of our patients. If our patient's mental health is adequately addressed, their physical health will be much easier to maintain. Thanks to my friend and colleague for making my work easier and my patients better citizens.

Dr. Jacqueline Stewart, *my former pediatrician, my children's pediatrician, my sister in Christ, my sorority sister, my friend, and my mentor*

PREFACE

It is my pleasure to present *SHINE: Understanding ADHD So Your Child Can Be a STAR!*

Early in my career as a child and adolescent psychiatrist, I realized that I would see attention deficit hyperactivity disorder (ADHD) more than any other mental illness in children. Soon after, I realized that educating concerned, exasperated, and overwhelmed parents, who were at their wits' end from their children's ADHD, would fill my workdays. I embraced the role I had and studied to provide my patients and their families with the best treatment possible. I found that most families presented similarly with only minor differences. I used the science of medicine to treat their similarities and the art of medicine to treat their differences. Soon, I found I was more than just the person prescribing medications. I was a part of the child's team of physicians, their family even. Even more, I realized I was a specialist, an expert, and my unique gift extended beyond helping hyperactive children remain in their seats.

My gift allows me to comfort confused moms and dads while educating them about ADHD with evidence-based medicine. I know what it takes for children to succeed, and my formula is here in print. My book will equip parents with the tools necessary to help their children be successful in the classroom and in life!

INTRODUCTION

Can you believe that when I was a little girl, I wanted to be a wife and mom most? (The dream to be a doctor came later!) I had it all planned: my children would sit, stop, and move only when I told them to, make Honor Roll, and sleep all night. It was going to be perfect, almost the way my dad and mom had it with me. And then I entered medicine.

I recall the first family I encountered whose child had ADHD. There was tension in the room between the parents, who disagreed on the diagnosis. The dad eventually stormed out the door, slamming it as he exited. And the mom was left, crying and sad, bear-hugging the child, who struggled to sit still to keep himself from breaking anything more in the room or from hurting himself. At that moment, I realized all mothers' experiences were not the ones I imagined, and my heart sank.

Then, I realized families did not have to live in the unpredictable world commonly seen in ADHD and that I could help them! By using my passion for treating ADHD and gifts of education, compassion, and wit, I began healing patients and their families. Now I hold my head high, knowing that I provide families with all the information and tools they need so they can advocate for, encourage, and empower their children. My goal is that my interaction with families will help catapult all children I impact toward ultimate success in the classroom and in life.

My prayer is that you will fully engage in this conversation, and that by its end, you too will have the confidence and knowledge needed to propel your child upwards toward the sun and to them being bright, shining stars.

CHAPTER ONE

Understanding ADHD

WHAT IS ADHD?

Attention deficit hyperactivity disorder (hereafter referred to as ADHD) is one of several disorders referred to as neurodevelopmental disorders. Neurodevelopmental disorders affect two things: the neurological system, which is made up of the brain and the spinal cord and impacts how the brain functions, and the child's development. The impact of neurodevelopmental disorders can vary greatly. Some only have mild impairments; persons with these disorders tend to live pretty typical lives without many limitations. Other neurodevelopmental disorders have significant impact and can require lifelong care from others besides the patient. Other examples of neurodevelopmental disorders besides ADHD include speech and language disorders, learning disorders, intellectual disorders, cerebral palsy, Tourette syndrome, fragile X syndrome, and even schizophrenia. Besides ADHD, the other most common neurodevelopmental disorder is autism spectrum disorder. All neurodevelopmental disorders have varying amounts of impact on the neurological system.

Besides having a neurological component, ADHD also has a developmental component, hence *developmental* in neurodevelopmental disorder. The impact is usually seen in young children as they are growing and developing. Sometimes you may notice symptoms as early as three years old. The disorder causes symptoms related to the nervous system and impacts behaviors. For this reason, it is sometimes called a neurobehavioral disorder, which accounts for the behaviors that can continue throughout the child's life and even into adulthood.

ADHD is a brain-based biological disorder. The brain is a complex organ that has many functions. It controls how we feel, think, and behave. It has long been known that there are differences in the brains of children with ADHD compared to children who do not have the disorder. Namely, children with ADHD have smaller brains than those without the disorder, but only by about 3%.[1] This alone does not impact a child's performance in the classroom or in life because we know that intelligence, or how "smart" a child is, is not determined by brain size.

We do know that in ADHD certain areas of the brain are more affected than others. The frontal lobe, located at the front of the brain, seems to be most involved in ADHD. The frontal lobe is the part of the brain that controls planning and carrying out tasks, organizing, focusing, making decisions, controlling impulsivity, delaying gratification, behaving appropriately in social situations, being motivated, creating memories, having time perception, and having impulse control. Besides actual lobe involvement, people with ADHD may also have neural pathways in some parts of their brains that are different from people who do not have ADHD. Some of these parts of the brain are also involved in attention, impulsive behaviors, motor activity, and inhibition. Even in typically developing children, disinhibition and risky behaviors can be the norm well into late adolescence or early adulthood. This is because the frontal lobe is the last part of the brain to develop and usually does not fully develop until a child ages into their mid-twenties.

ADHD is a common neurobehavioral disorder of childhood. The Centers for Disease Control and Prevention (CDC) reports that 11% of American school-age children have ADHD. This includes children 4 to 17 years old. This number is nearly double what it was eight years ago. About 6% of American children are being treated for ADHD with medication. And even though it presents and is diagnosed in early childhood, about 4% of American adults over the age of 18 years old still have ADHD symptoms.[2]

WHAT CAUSES ADHD?

By definition, a mental illness is any disorder that impacts your child's behavior, thinking, sleeping, eating, learning, or mood. ADHD is one of the most extensively studied mental illnesses affecting children. Despite being extensively studied, research has failed to show any one cause for ADHD and instead has shown that there can be multiple causes for ADHD. In fact, we say that the causes of ADHD are multifactorial. This means it is caused by many ("multi") things ("factors"). Some causes of ADHD are related to the child's genes or things happening when the mom is carrying the baby. Other causes are related to the environment. Still, other causes are related to neurologic, or brain, abnormalities that the child may have.

Before we discuss the genetic component of ADHD, let us define some key words and definitions.

- *Genetics* is the general term used to discuss the idea that genes make up every living cell. In this theory, genes give the instruction for how our bodies are to grow and develop. A genetic condition is not necessarily a hereditary disorder. An example of this is achondroplasia, which has dwarfism as a primary feature. Even though it is a genetic disorder, it is not hereditary because parents of typical height can have children who are dwarfs.

- *Hereditary* indicates that something is passed from parent to child. A hereditary disorder is a genetic disorder. An example of a hereditary trait is eye color.

- *Familial* describes a trait that family members have in common. An example is diabetes, which tends to run in families but does not have a specific genetic cause.

The best information we have now suggests that ADHD is a genetic disorder. Genetics accounts for 70–80% of the causes of ADHD.[3] The genetics are complicated, though, because several different genes contribute only a small amount of risk. And while ADHD is known to "run in families" and is largely thought to be genetic, no specific gene has been identified as a cause.

Here is what is known about the genetic component: 41% of mothers and 51% of fathers with ADHD pass the disorder on to their children.[4] Siblings of children with ADHD are more likely to have the disorder, and twins are even more likely to be affected than siblings, in general.

Besides genetics, events that happen during and immediately after your pregnancy and around the time of your child's birth can lead to ADHD. The risk factor with the strongest evidence for ADHD may be low birth weight, which often is the result of premature delivery (preterm birth). Babies born "very" and "extremely" preterm or at very and extremely low birth weights are much more likely to develop ADHD than children born full term at typical weights. Legal and commonly used substances that may have been used during pregnancy, such as cigarettes and alcohol, are risk factors for ADHD. Likewise, illicit substances that may have been used during pregnancy, like cocaine and methamphetamine, can also lead to premature birth and low birth weight, which are known risks for ADHD. Lastly, trauma to the mother's abdomen is thought to have some impact on the likelihood of an unborn child having ADHD.

Environmental exposures have also been identified as risk factors for ADHD. Lead is one example of an environmental substance that can lead to ADHD. Lead is commonly found in lead-based paints. Homes built in the United States prior to 1978 are likely to have some lead-based paint. When the paint peels and cracks, it makes lead paint chips and dust. Children ingest those chips of paint, and this can cause many different symptoms consistent with lead toxicity, including gastrointestinal (GI) and neurologic symptoms, like constipation and pain in the abdomen, headaches, irritability, tingling in the hands and feet, and symptoms of ADHD.

Polychlorinated biphenyls (PCBs) are other environmental substances that can lead to ADHD. PCBs, banned in 1979, are a group of man-made chemicals that were used in electrical equipment. They are still present in many products that were made before they were banned. PCBs seem to make it difficult for children to show response inhibition.

There are suggestions of a possible link between ADHD and pesticides but this is not well studied. Certain impacts to the neurologic system and neurologic disorders can cause ADHD. One such disorder is epilepsy, which is a seizure disorder. Patients with epilepsy are three times more likely to have ADHD than those who do not.[6] Trauma to the brain, whether caused during pregnancy or a head injury later in life, can lead to ADHD symptoms. Know that no matter the cause of ADHD, extremely effective treatments exist.

WHAT DOES NOT CAUSE ADHD?

While several toxins and behavioral and environmental conditions have been thought to cause ADHD, some continue to lack research support and therefore are not considered to cause the disorder. Some examples of things that DO NOT cause ADHD are too much sugar, dietary components, too much television or video games, "bad parenting," poverty, and family chaos. (See Chapter 4: "Treating ADHD.")

WHO GETS ADHD?

The average age for presentation of symptoms of ADHD is typically between 3 and 6 years old. The average age of diagnosis is 7 years old. According to the Centers for Disease Control and Prevention (CDC), the total estimated number of children diagnosed with ADHD as of 2016 was 6.1 million (9.4%). This number includes 388,000 (15%) children ages 2–5 years old, 4 million children ages 6–11 years old, and 3 million children ages 12–17 years old. In all, 11% of American children between 4 and 7 years old have ADHD. In this same 2016 report, 77% of children with ADHD were receiving some form of treatment. While most parents consider ADHD a diagnosis of childhood only, the diagnosis among adults is growing four times faster than are ADHD diagnoses among children in the USA. Despite this, it is still thought that ADHD in adults is underdiagnosed.[7]

There has been a 42% increase in ADHD diagnoses over the past eight years.[2] While there is a known increase in the number of people diagnosed with ADHD, the reason for this increase is not clear. It is worth mentioning and clarifying, however, that ADHD has always been present. We know this because parents and sometimes grandparents of children who are diagnosed endorse having had symptoms when they were children and even as adults. So, it is less likely that ADHD has increased, and more likely that those diagnosing the disorder are more aware of the symptoms required for the diagnosis and are more comfortable with making it.[5]

Many people speculate that ADHD is "over-diagnosed" but research continues to show that the diagnosis is most often applied correctly. Some note an increase in health care access as an explanation for the increase in ADHD's diagnosis and credit the Affordable Care Act (ACA), commonly called "Obamacare," with widening access to care, especially among minority and lower-income communities. However, an increase in awareness of the disorder, especially in the ways the disorder presents differently in boys and girls, and the gradually decreasing stigma related to ADHD are factors that contribute to an increase in the diagnosis. Now teachers and parents are aware of the symptoms and this leads to parents often asking pediatricians about the disorder. Also, doctors are better trained to recognize the symptoms and make the diagnosis than they were 20 years ago.[5] More likely, the increase in the number of cases is related to a better understanding of the disorder and what its diagnostic criteria are.[8]

Regarding race and ADHD, there is not much difference in the rate that different racial and cultural groups have the disorder. However, diagnosis and treatment do differ significantly based on race.[9] (The National Survey of Children's Health [NSCH] showed less than 5 percentage points difference between Blacks, whites, non-Hispanic Latino, Hispanic Latino, and persons who identified their race as other.[10]) Some articles report that blacks are diagnosed with ADHD more than whites, while other articles report the opposite. Most articles report that Hispanics are diagnosed less frequently than whites or blacks. Some reasons that would explain blacks being diagnosed less often than whites include poor access to care or mistrust of the medical system due to inappropriate medical treatment of blacks in the past and even in the news now.[9]

According to the CDC, boys are three times more likely to be diagnosed with ADHD than are girls.[7] This is most likely because ADHD symptoms present differently in boys and girls. Boys tend to be more hyperactive and aggressive and these symptoms usually get parents' and teachers' attention much earlier than girls' behaviors, which tend to be more subtle and sometimes can be harder to identify. Boys tend to show externalized symptoms, such as running and impulsivity, whereas girls with ADHD typically show internalized symptoms, like inattentiveness and low self-esteem. Boys also tend to be more physically aggressive, whereas girls tend to be more verbally aggressive. In fact, it is the talkativeness that is a key feature of girls with ADHD and leads to them being called "Chatty Cathys." Girls' talkativeness is much more common than their being hyperactive. Boys tend to externalize their frustrations with anger and aggression, but girls usually turn their pain and anger inward. This puts girls at increased risk for depression, anxiety, and eating disorders, which usually become noticeable by middle school. Girls with undiagnosed ADHD are more likely to have problems in school, social settings, and personal relationships than other girls. On the other hand, boys with untreated ADHD are likely to have problems with aggression and defiant behaviors, and these could result in problems with the law.[11]

Regarding treatment, 62% of children with ADHD are currently taking ADHD medication. This is further broken down into 18.2% of children with ADHD ages 2–5, 68.6% of children with ADHD ages 6–11, and 62.1% of children with ADHD ages 12–17.[1]

SPOTLIGHT

The causes of ADHD are multifactorial. There is no one cause of the disorder.

The treatment for ADHD is very effective and can lead to success in the classroom and in life.

CHAPTER TWO

Diagnosing ADHD

THE ROLE OF THE DSM IN THE DIAGNOSIS OF ADHD

The American Psychiatric Association's Diagnostic and Statistical Manual, Fifth Edition (DSM-5) provides guidelines for diagnosing ADHD and all other mental illnesses. The criteria in the DSM-5 makes diagnosing mental illnesses standard among providers. (Recall that a mental illness is any disorder that impacts your child's behavior, thinking, sleeping, eating, learning, or mood, so, by definition, ADHD is a mental illness.) By making it standard, doctors and others can be assured that the numbers of children affected by ADHD and the assessment and reporting of the impact ADHD has on the public remain consistent. (Please note that for consistency, "doctor" will be used throughout the book. However, for a full list of specialists who can provide mental health diagnoses and treatment, see the "Who Can Diagnose ADHD?" section later in this chapter.)

The DSM-5 lists three types of ADHD: predominantly inattentive presentation, predominantly hyperactive-impulsive presentation, and combined presentation. Each is based on the symptoms the child has. Children who meet criteria for the predominantly inattentive presentation of ADHD must have most of these symptoms: they cannot maintain focus and are easily distracted, lose things, procrastinate, are forgetful, are disorganized, seem "spaced out" and do not respond when addressed, they cannot complete tasks, and they rush through activities often making careless mistakes.

Children who meet criteria for the predominantly hyperactive-impulsive presentation of ADHD must have most of these symptoms: cannot stay seated, are talkative and loud, blurt and interrupt when others are talking, fidget, are always on the go and always running and jumping, and cannot wait their turn.

Children who only have significant inattentive symptoms are diagnosed with *predominantly inattentive presentation*. Children who only have significant hyperactive and impulsive symptoms are diagnosed with *predominantly hyperactive-impulsive presentation*. And children who have significant inattentive and hyperactive-impulsive symptoms are diagnosed with *combined presentation*.

It is not enough for the child to meet the symptom criteria above. The child must also have had several symptoms before 12yo, must have symptoms in at least two settings (like school and home or school and grandmother's house), and must have some reduction in his or her ability to enjoy or function at school, social settings, or work. The doctor will also rule out mental health diagnoses that can mimic ADHD and will make diagnoses that are known to commonly occur with ADHD. (See Chapter 5: "Treating Comorbid Disorders of ADHD.") Regardless of the presentation, symptoms must be present for the six months just before diagnosis. Both children and adults can be diagnosed with ADHD. Adults need fewer symptoms to get the diagnosis than children, but adults can receive the diagnosis even if they have not been diagnosed in the past.

Some parents may recall there being an ADD diagnosis, which did not include hyperactive and impulsive symptoms. This often prompts the question, "What is the difference between ADD and ADHD?" "ADD" is no longer a recognized diagnosis. However, it is closest in meaning to ADHD, predominantly inattentive presentation.

HOW IS ADHD DIAGNOSED?

ADHD is a clinical diagnosis and is made, in very large part, based on clinical interview and observation. That means that, except in some very rare and special cases, no blood tests or imaging studies of the brain are routinely recommended. Instead, clinical interview and observation are the most important aspects of diagnosing ADHD and other diagnostic tests (like blood work and imaging studies of the brain) can be recommended based on history and physical findings. Parents are often the first to suspect ADHD symptoms. Sometimes this comes at the insistence of teachers and others in the school or other structured setting. The pediatrician or family practitioner is usually the first person to make a diagnosis or act on parents' suspicion of the diagnosis. He or she may then refer to a developmental pediatrician, a psychologist, or psychiatrist for further testing, diagnostic clarification, and treatment. In large part, your report as the child's parents is heavily relied upon because often children cannot verbalize their behaviors and/or because they lack insight (the ability to recognize their symptoms).

A key component of the evaluation of ADHD includes the thorough history-taking of biological, psychological, and social histories. This is often referred to as the BIO-PSYCHO-SOCIAL history approach. The biological part of the evaluation includes a thorough history of the events of your pregnancy, delivery, and the period just after birth; any illnesses, surgeries, and drugs (prescription, street, or illicit) you used while pregnant; and your age at delivery. Information about adoption should be mentioned, if applicable. The psychological history should include pertinent medical, psychiatric, and substance use histories in family members and the child. The social history should include the number, age, and relation of all persons who live with the patient; information about any history in foster care or being out of your care (or their biological parent's care); the child's academic history, any special education services, truancy issues, and disciplinary actions; and the child's legal or illegal substance use history.

A physical exam should be considered a standard part of any ADHD diagnostic work-up. The primary care physician (pediatrician or family medicine doctor) may complete this exam, but the results should be shared with the diagnosing mental health specialist. The physical examination and other key parts of the medical history can give significant tips about medical conditions that may lead to or co-occur with ADHD. Medical conditions should always be considered and ruled out before a diagnosis of ADHD is given, even though they can occur along with ADHD.

Certain general medical conditions and their treatments, neurologic conditions, psychiatric conditions, and environmental conditions can all mimic ADHD or occur in combination with ADHD. For example, poor vision and hearing deficits are medical conditions that can lead to inattention. Certain treatments for asthma have long been thought to lead to hyperactivity. Neurologic conditions, such as seizure disorders, can be associated with ADHD. Psychiatric conditions like anxiety and depression can appear as and co-occur with ADHD. And environmental conditions such as dysfunctional and stressful home environments, gifted or learning-disabled school environments, and mental illness in parents could all be confounders that look like ADHD. (See Chapter 6: "Advocating for Your Child With ADHD.")

Because there are so many things to consider in the differential (list of diagnoses the child could have in addition to or instead of ADHD), it may take several sessions before all diagnoses are confirmed.[12]

The diagnosis of ADHD requires symptoms to be present in at least two environments. These can include home and school, home and church, home and grandmother's house, or church and school, as examples. Often, teachers and others who work with the child inside and outside of the home can complete symptom rating scales to report behaviors in the setting where they work with the child. However, it is important to note that sometimes teachers may not notice symptoms in the classroom and subsequently under-report on the rating scales. This may be because subconsciously they are comparing the patient to the other students and find that the patient's behaviors "are not as bad as" other students so they minimize the symptoms they report. Also, other, more veteran, teachers may believe that patients are "just typical boys," for example, and do not believe their behaviors are outside of the norm. On the contrary, parents sometimes do not notice symptoms at home even after teachers report symptoms at school. This may speak to some behavioral modifications parents use that teachers cannot, like spanking, or to the fact that parents are often more tolerable of children's behaviors than teachers can be when there are other students in the classroom.

RATING SCALES FOR ADHD

Rating scales are a key part of the assessment of ADHD. They can be used to help screen, evaluate, and monitor symptoms of ADHD. Scales are useful in making the diagnosis of ADHD, but they cannot and should not be used alone. (Alone, rating scales do not provide enough information to make a diagnosis.) Once the diagnosis has been made and treatment begun, rating scales can also be used to monitor the child's progress. Rating scales typically ask the adult who is completing the rating scale to score the child's behaviors, usually on a 0–3 or 4-point scale, where 0 means never and 3 or 4 means very often. A higher score correlates with more severe symptoms.

Table 1: Screening vs. Assessment Tools

Screening	Assessment
❯ Can give warning of possible problem	❯ Specifies a problem, if one is present
❯ Can have multiple question types, like yes/no or 0-4	❯ Correlates with DSM-5 diagnosis
❯ Suggests if further evaluation is needed	❯ Can be used to create treatment plan
❯ Should not be used alone to make a diagnosis	❯ Person administrating may require special degrees and/or training

ADHD rating scales are available for children, teenagers, and even adults. They can be very short and take as little as five minutes to complete. Or they can take 20 minutes to complete. Each rating scale asks diagnostic criteria for ADHD and commonly co-occurring disorders, like oppositional defiant disorder (ODD), conduct disorder, mood disorders, and anxiety disorders. Some also allow for reports about the child's interactions with peers and academic performance. A version of the Vanderbilt I have created for my practice has lines for teachers to write free text, and it specifically asks about times of day the rater works with the child. This information can be used for both diagnostic and treatment response purposes.

When compared to each other, rating scales can provide insight into reasons that a child may appear inattentive in class or why a child may not be performing well academically. For example, if rating scales reveal that a child who takes medications for ADHD focuses in all morning classes but is inattentive in all afternoon classes, this child's medications may be wearing off prematurely and medication adjustments may be necessary. However, if a child focuses well between 8am and 10am, cannot focus between 10am and 11am, and focuses well between 11am and 3pm, this points away from inattention as the primary explanation and should lead school officials and parents to search for other explanations. Some possible reasons for this discrepancy in a child's ability to focus one hour in the middle of the day include difficulty with the subject matter (a learning disorder), interpersonal difficulties with the teacher, bullying, and even a mid-morning fatigue from poorly sleeping the night before.

Among physicians, two of the most popular ADHD rating scales for children include the:

- National Institute for Children's Health Quality (NICHQ) Vanderbilt Assessment Scale, for children ages 6 to 12. The Vanderbilt is readily available for download on the internet at no cost. There are two forms of the Vanderbilt: one for parents and one for teachers. The questions on both versions align with diagnostic criteria for ADHD as they are listed in the DSM-5. The parent assessment scale has a separate section for conduct disorder, or antisocial behavior, while the teacher assessment scale has an extra section for recording information about the child's academic performance.

- Conners Comprehensive Behavior Rating Scale (CBRS), for children ages 6 to 18. Unlike the Vanderbilt, the Conners has an associated cost that the clinician usually covers. In addition to being used to alert clinicians to the presence of ADHD, the Conners CBRS is designed to determine if students meet criteria for special education services. Like the Vanderbilt, there are parent and teacher forms. When the Conners is repeated over time, clinicians can determine if symptoms are improving and if the treatment plan is effective.

There are several other rating scales that can suggest ADHD and other behavioral problems. Your child's doctor will suggest them as needed.

Comparison of Vanderbilt and Conners Scales[13]

Scale	Free	Multiple Informants	Ages	Screens for Comorbid Conditions	Validated with Norms	Items
Vanderbilt	Yes	Yes	6-12	Yes	No	26-55
Conners	No	Yes	3-17	Yes	Yes	59-87 37 (short)

WHO CAN DIAGNOSE ADHD?

ADHD can be diagnosed by psychologists and neuropsychologists; physicians, including general pediatricians, developmental-behavioral pediatricians, psychiatrists, child and adolescent psychiatrists, family practitioners, and neurologists; advanced practice registered nurses (APRN)/certified registered nurse practitioners (CRNPs), and physician assistants; counselors, social workers, and other licensed counselors or therapists; and educational (school) psychometrists. Let us discuss each of these:

- A *psychologist/neuropsychologist* has a terminal degree, which is usually a PhD (Doctor of Philosophy) or a PsyD (Doctor of Psychology). He or she is called "doctor." A psychologist's training typically consists of four years of college, two years of graduate school to obtain a master's degree, and four to six years of a doctoral program, followed by one to two years of full-time internship. (Neuropsychologists have more training beyond this.) A psychologist or neuropsychologist can make a diagnosis of ADHD by using clinical evaluation and by using psychological testing. A psychologist cannot prescribe medications.

- A *physician* also has a terminal degree, which is most commonly an MD (Medical Doctor) or DO (Doctor of Osteopathic Medicine) in the United States. He or she is called "doctor." All medical doctors have unrestricted ability to prescribe medications.

A physician's training typically consists of four years of college, four years of medical school, and a variable number of years in residency depending on the specialty as outlined here:

- A *general pediatrician* completes a three-year residency in pediatrics. He or she can diagnose ADHD using clinical evaluation but cannot administer psychological testing. General pediatricians can prescribe medications.

- A *developmental-behavioral pediatrician (DBP)* completes a three-year residency in pediatrics and then completes an extra period of training, called a fellowship, in development behavioral pediatrics. This fellowship is three years. DBPs are trained to consider both medical and psychological aspects of a child's development and behavior and to treat atypical presentations as they arise. As such, a DBP can diagnose ADHD using clinical evaluation but cannot administer psychological testing. Developmental-behavioral pediatricians can prescribe medications.

- A *psychiatrist* completes a four-year psychiatry residency. He or she usually will see adults only but can see children. A psychiatrist can make a diagnosis of ADHD by using clinical evaluation and by using psychological testing, although most psychiatrists who are not associated with a university setting do not usually administer psychological tests. Psychiatrists can prescribe medications.

- A *child and adolescent psychiatrist (CAP)* completes a four-year psychiatry residency and then completes an extra period of training, called a fellowship, where they learn how to treat younger patients. A CAP's fellowship lasts between one and two years. A child and adolescent psychiatrist can make a diagnosis of ADHD by using clinical evaluation and by using psychological testing, although most child and adolescent psychiatrists who are not associated with a university setting do not usually administer psychological tests. Psychiatrists can prescribe medications.

- A *family practitioner* completes a three-year residency in family medicine. He or she receives training in obstetrics, pediatrics, general surgery, emergency medicine, and inpatient hospital care (including critical care) and can diagnose ADHD using clinical evaluation but cannot administer psychological testing. Family practitioners can prescribe medications.

- A *neurologist* completes a four-year neurology residency. Some neurologists complete an extra period of training, called a fellowship, where they learn how to treat a specific patient population. However, *pediat-*

ric neurologists typically complete one to two years of general pediatrics residency, then three years of residency training in pediatric neurology, which includes one year of training in adult neurology. Neurologists can diagnose ADHD using clinical evaluation but cannot administer psychological testing. Neurologists can prescribe medications.

- A *certified registered nurse practitioner (CRNP)* is one of the four types of Advanced Practice Registered Nurse (APRN). (The other three types are Clinical Nurse Specialist [CNS], Certified Registered Nurse Anesthetist [CRNA], and Certified Nurse-Midwife [CNM].) A CRNP has at least a Master of Science in Nursing (MSN). A CRNP is NOT called "doctor." Some CRNPs have earned a Doctor of Nursing Practice (DNP) or a PhD in nursing and can be called "doctor" because of this degree but are not medical doctors. (Think of how psychologists are called "doctor" because of their terminal degree but are not medical doctors.) CRNPs can diagnose ADHD using clinical evaluation but cannot administer psychological testing. CRNPs can prescribe medications but they may have restrictions on the type/class of medications they can prescribe based on their state and the number of years they have been out of school.

- A *physician assistant* has a master's degree. A physician assistant is not called "doctor." Their training consists of four years of college and then roughly two years of graduate school to earn a master's degree. Physician assistants can diagnose ADHD. They can prescribe medications but may have restrictions on the type/class of medication they can prescribe based on their state and the number of years they have been out of school.

- A *counselor* has a master's degree, usually in counseling. A counselor is not called "doctor." Their training consists of four years of college and then two years of graduate school to obtain a master's degree. They can diagnose ADHD using clinical evaluation but cannot administer psychological testing. They cannot prescribe medications. Instead, counselors help families and individuals work through specific problems or mental illnesses, usually for a specific amount of time.

- A *social worker* has a master's degree, usually in social work. A social worker is not called "doctor." Their training consists of four years of college, two years of graduate school to obtain a master's degree, then two to three years of supervised clinical work. In addition to counseling, social workers can help patients connect to services they may need in the community, such as locating sources for housing, medications, transportation, and employment. They can diagnose ADHD using clinical evaluation but cannot administer psychological testing. They cannot prescribe medications.

- A *psychometrist* has at least a bachelor's degree. Some have master's degrees, but this is not always required. A psychometrist is not called "doctor." Their training consists of at least four years of college and then another two years of graduate school to earn a master's degree, if they choose to pursue one. Psychometrists have specialized training in administering and scoring various tests that assess neuropsychological and psychological functioning. Psychometrists work under the supervision of a licensed psychologist or neuropsychologist. Psychometrists can diagnose ADHD using psychological testing. They cannot prescribe medications.

Table 2: Who Can Diagnose, Treat, and Provide Therapy for ADHD?

	Psychologist	Psychometrist	Physician***	CRNP	Physician assistant	Social worker	Therapist
Degree	PhD/PsyD	Masters	MD/DO	Masters	Masters	Masters	Masters
"DOCTOR"?	YES	NO	YES	NO	NO	NO	NO
Can diagnose?	YES	YES	YES	YES	YES	YES	YES
Can administer testing?	YES	YES	YES	NO	NO	NO	NO
Can prescribe?	NO	YES	YES	YES	YES	NO	NO
Talk therapy?	YES	YES	Variable	Variable	NO	YES	YES

*** Medical doctors include general pediatricians, behavioral pediatricians, family practitioners, (child and adolescent) psychiatrists, and neurologists.

Table 3: Which Type of Doctor Provides Talk Therapy?

Medical specialty	Provides therapy typically?
Psychiatrist/Child and Adolescent Psychiatrist	YES
General pediatrician	NO
Behavioral pediatrician	NO
Family practitioner	NO
Neurologist	NO

PSYCHOLOGICAL TESTING

There are two types of testing that can be used to diagnose ADHD, though neither of them is necessarily required. (Recall that ADHD is a clinical diagnosis, meaning that patient exam, reports from the patient and his or her parents, and rating scales from teachers and others who work with the child are most often sufficient to make the diagnosis.) Psychologists and neuropsychologists administer psychological and neuropsychological tests. These tests are standardized, which means they are administered the same way and under the same conditions every time. Both forms of testing can be especially useful as a part of treatment planning, particularly for educational purposes, but the details they reveal are different. Both types of tests deeply review the patient's birth, developmental, medical, family, social, and psychological history and combine reports from the patient's parents, teachers, doctors, and therapists. However, they differ in their overall goal: psychological tests determine IF a disorder is present, while neuropsychological tests determine WHY a disorder is present.

Typical standard psychological/diagnostic evaluations are often used to diagnose neurodevelopmental disorders, like ADHD and autism spectrum disorder, or psychiatric disorders, like mood, anxiety, behavioral, and psychotic disorders. Psychologists include cognitive testing, to include IQ and achievement testing; evaluation of emotional function, to include assessing for depression, anxiety, deficits in identity formation, sleep disorders, personality functioning, and obtaining data regarding developmental and emotional age and family dynamics; evaluation of behavioral function, to include evaluation of substance abuse, trauma abuse, risk for self-harm, aggression, and treatment compliance, and rule out thought disorders and screen for organic impairment; executive functioning assessment, to include accountability, self-regulation, problem-solving, planning, organizing, inhibition, meta-cognition (self-awareness), communication, and working memory.

Neuropsychologists use testing that focuses more on disorders that are thought to have a brain or neurologic basis.

Neuropsychology looks at all aspects of the child, including their genetic, developmental, and environmental histories, and uses these to explain the child's presentation. Neuropsychological tests can be used when there is a known or suspected neurological disorder (like seizures), injuries (like force to the head that may cause concussion), environmental exposures (like lead poisoning, or prenatal exposure to alcohol or drugs), and other factors that may lead to neurological deficits (like prematurity or other pregnancy-related problems). Neuropsychological tests can also be used to evaluate complex neurodevelopmental disorders, like ADHD, dyslexia, autism spectrum disorder, and nonverbal learning disorder.

While standard psychological testing can be used to diagnose a condition like ADHD based upon behavior, neuropsychological testing can specify the origin, severity, and development of a disorder and then can be used to customize recommendations to create a specific treatment plan.

Building upon the standard evaluation, neuropsychological evaluations assess: attention and concentration; memory (verbal and visual); functioning (visual-spatial functioning and executive); gross and fine motor development; sensory integration; audiology and phonology; and language and reading skills.[15]

There are several types of neuropsychological assessments. Some of the more common ones are:

- Woodcock-Johnson Test of Cognitive Abilities
- Wechsler Individual Achievement Test (WIAT)
- Nelson-Denny Reading Test
- Wechsler Intelligence Scale for Children (WISC-V)

To be clear, ADHD is a clinical diagnosis. However, if there ever is a question about the diagnosis or if the child is not improving with an appropriate treatment plan, then psychological testing is the gold standard to determine if ADHD or any psychological disorder is present. It may take several days to complete psychological and neuropsychological testing, but the combination of tests will give clear, thorough diagnoses of all mental illnesses, including ADHD.

CONTINUOUS PERFORMANCE TESTS

Continuous Performance Tests (CPTs) can also be a part of a thorough evaluation for ADHD, but they are not required. CPTs assess a child's ability to remain focused during a non-entertaining task and to control their impulses during an exciting task. (Recall that ADHD is comprised of symptoms of inattention, hyperactivity, and impulsivity.) These tests are objective, which means they are free of examiner (doctor) bias.

The Test of Variables of Attention (T.O.V.A.) is one example of a CPT. It is a computerized standardized test that uses visual and auditory (hearing) components to help diagnose ADHD and monitor the effect of medications in a child who has ADHD. Some of the variables that the T.O.V.A measures include: response time (how fast the child responds to a target), signal detection (how quickly the child's performance worsens during the T.O.V.A. assessment), commission errors (how many times the child presses the switch in response to a non-target; this measures impulsivity), omission errors (how many times the child does not press the switch in response to a target; this measures inattention), multiple responses (which measure the number of times a child activates their micro-switch more than once when a target is shown; this may suggest other neurological conditions), and anticipatory responses (which measure how often the patient is pressing the switch so quickly that they may be guessing). The test usually lasts 21.6 minutes for children 6 years and older, and 10.8 minutes for children who are between 4 and 5 years old. In the visual test, children are shown several targets and non-targets, which are geometric stimuli. They are told to respond to a certain target with a micro-switch or to not respond when a non-target is shown. In the auditory test, your child is exposed to two tones that represent the target and non-target. He or she will then press the micro- switch when the target tone sounds and will not press the switch when the non-target tone sounds.[16]

The T.O.V.A. assessment is not used as frequently as it was in the past because it does not collect enough data to give a diagnosis of ADHD. In fact, the company that makes the T.O.V.A states that it cannot be used alone to make a diagnosis of ADHD.

SPOTLIGHT

A terminal degree is the highest degree available in a specific academic discipline. A terminal degree is called a "doctorate" and people who have earned one are called "doctors."

Psycholo**GIST**s get the **GIST** of medications but cannot prescribe them.

Medical doctors can have either an MD or a DO. They both complete four years of medical school and then complete a residency program. Doctors who have a DO often spend extra time studying a holistic approach to medicine and have spent extra time learning hands-on techniques.

Psychia**TR**ists **TR**eat ADHD with medications.

"A career in healthcare is a commitment to preventing disease, promoting well-being, and doing no harm; both nurse practitioners and medical doctors embrace an ethos of service, knowledge, teamwork, flexibility, compassion, and safety, but there are key differences in the two occupations in terms of experience, education, and credentialing."[14]

Certified Registered Nurse Practitioners (CRNPs) are nurses, even if they have a doctorate/terminal degree and can be called "doctor."

Psychologists, therapists, and social workers can all provide talk therapy, but their training, approach, and overall goals may all be different.

Psychological testing is the gold standard for diagnosing mental health disorders but is not always necessary to make diagnoses.

ADHD is primarily a clinical diagnosis. It only requires physical evaluation, observation, and interview of the patient; a detailed review of the birth, developmental, medical, family, and social histories; and interview of the parents, especially when children are unable to give a history. Any additional radiographic or psychological evaluations are not necessary but can be helpful if the initial evaluations do not give a clear diagnosis or there is concern for other medical and/or psychological diagnoses. Complementary tests, like Continuous Performance Tests, are also not necessary, and, in fact, may only help to confirm a diagnosis but alone cannot determine the diagnosis.

Alone, rating scales do not provide enough information to make a diagnosis.

Having several, if not all, teachers complete rating scales and note the times they interact with the child is key for determining if ADHD symptoms or some other problem is the best explanation for your child's presentation.

Children with ADHD are widely known to have associated, specific learning disorders. Generally, boys tend to have reading disorders and girls tend to have math disorders, but this is not always the case.

CHAPTER THREE

The Changing Faces of ADHD: Knowing How It Presents

HOW DOES ADHD USUALLY PRESENT?

As a parent, you may be the first person to notice symptoms of hyperactivity in your child, sometimes as early as between three and six years old. Or, someone else may bring the symptoms to your attention. For example, your child's daycare may be the first to notice symptoms when they mention them to you.

Despite the age at which you may recognize symptoms in your child, the average age for ADHD diagnosis is not until seven years old. The delay in average age of diagnosis may be for several reasons. Firstly, by age seven, parents have recognized the behaviors teachers have reported and they are more likely to consider the child's behaviors as atypical and different from other, non-hyperactive children. Secondly, there can be a delay in girls' diagnoses because their behaviors, which are less likely to include significant hyperactivity and aggression compared to boys, tends to be less obvious to teachers and other adults. Thirdly, by seven years, children are likely to have failed or come close to failing a grade in school and parents fear a second failure. Fourthly, families may have experienced difficulties arranging childcare as the child's hyperactivity and disruptive behaviors are deterrents for relatives and friends who would otherwise babysit.

The age at which your child presents for treatment can be thought of as being inversely related to the severity of symptoms. The younger a child is at presentation and diagnosis is most likely to indicate a significant level of disruptive and hyperactive behaviors. Contrarily, children with less hyperactivity tend to be diagnosed later in childhood years.

Over your child's lifespan, the main presentation of ADHD may change. Of course, all symptoms of ADHD can be present at any time, but there are certain times when some symptoms cause more challenges than others. For example, hyperactivity presents a major challenge in very young children. Inattention presents major challenges, especially academically, in children who are in the middle of childhood. And impulsivity causes more concerns in older children and adolescents. Of note, impulsive behaviors tend to extend into adulthood and can cause social and safety challenges, but inattention can also cause challenges for the adult, especially related to maintaining employment.

When your child is very young, perhaps up to about third grade, you and his or her teachers may complain about **hyperactivity most**. Children this young often cannot stay in their seats, often roll on the floor, are loud, twirl or chew holes in their clothes, and cannot be still long enough to learn. Often, children will fail a grade between kindergarten and third grade, but this is most likely due to their hyperactivity preventing them from sitting long enough to attend and learn and less likely due to their ability to learn. Some students with hyperactivity enter school without standard kindergarten readiness knowledge because their hyperactivity prevented them learning in pre-kindergarten years. This is especially true when children have been asked to not return to daycare or pre-kindergarten because of their disruptive behaviors.

By third grade, **inattention** is the symptom that causes most parents, like you, the most concern. In this grade two significant things happen. Developmentally, children have calmed and are not as hyperactive as they were in the past, and there is also a shift in academics that requires children to apply what they are reading and learning, often in real time. This means that children's bodies may be quietly staying in their seats but their brains continue to move nonstop. Teachers may be more focused on the other children who are still very hyperactive, and this may lead to your child's inattention going unnoticed. Many parents and other professionals do not understand this change and think the more "well-behaved" child cannot have ADHD because of the absence of overt hyperactivity. Academically, you may continue to applaud your child's ability to "read" before third grade but may find that he or she cannot "concentrate" by the time they are in the middle of the third grade, the year many will fail. For example, prior to third grade, your child's ability to say the words "See Joe run" were met with excitement. But by third grade the child may seem confused if the teacher asks, as a follow-up, "How was Joe moving?" You may find that your child cannot answer the question because he or she only called the words out loud and was not actually comprehending what was printed. It is not just third grade that can prove to be challenging. All odd-numbered grades can prove to be challenging for the child with ADHD as these are years when curricula change, preparation for standardized tests is common, and requirements for true focus increase.

The child in early elementary can be very irritable and emotional. This irritability stems, in large part, from the frustration that results from consistently not completing tasks, not scoring what they feel they should have on schoolwork, or for being in trouble with their parents, likely because of one of these things or for something similar. Parents' frustrations counter the child's frustration, and children's disruptive behaviors and poor academic performance snowball into a never-ending cycle that eventually ends in symptoms consistent with oppositional defiant disorder (ODD). (See Chapter 5: "Treating Comorbid Disorders of ADHD.") Treating the ADHD symptoms, which is usually the basis of all the discord, makes the emotionality better and disrupts the cycle—and leads to peace in the home again.

By middle school, **impulsivity** becomes more of a concern. Adolescents are allowed more developmentally appropriate freedoms, which means that they are away from their parents and are alone, sometimes unsupervised, with their peers. This could lead to more risky behaviors, like experimenting with drugs, sexual intercourse, and recklessness while driving a vehicle. Of note, these things more typically occur after school, on weekends, and when school is out for summer, fall, and winter breaks. These are also the times when many parents honor "medication holidays" and do not give their children medications. But these can also be the times a child is most in the position to be injured, engage in risky behaviors, or even be killed. All of these can further lead to lifelong struggles with drugs, sexual promiscuity and teenage pregnancy, moving vehicle violations and motor vehicle accidents, and even death.

For the high school student, impulsivity can appear in adolescents' driving. Without treatment, adolescents with ADHD change lanes without checking for a car on their side while driving. They also overestimate their ability to make it through a yellow light and either crash into another car or get a moving vehicle violation. If not one of these things, they drive more than the speed limit and get a moving vehicle violation, or they have a single vehicle accident, often with a stationary item, like a tree. As inattention continues to be a problem and the level of difficulty and volume of schoolwork increases, adolescents eventually become overwhelmed with their academics and may eventually drop out of high school. In fact, roughly 33% of children with ADHD do not complete high school compared to 4% of comparisons, and only 4% had higher degrees compared with 29% of comparisons.[18]

Moodiness can be present throughout the lifespan of the child with ADHD but you may notice that it can begin to take the form of frank depression and anxiety as the child enters adolescence. During adolescence children with ADHD may appear irritable, isolate in their rooms, and appear to have a change in sleeping patterns. Or they may be anxious, but only on school days or around academically-related activities. Some girls have been known to vomit as they near the school building or even the street where the school is located. On clinical interview, these adolescents often do not meet criteria for major depressive disorder or generalized anxiety disorder. (However, sometimes they do.) Instead, they are much more likely to meet criteria for ADHD, which has gone unnoticed, undiagnosed, and unchecked since early elementary school, if not earlier.

About 60% of children with ADHD will have symptoms into adulthood. Total, about 4% to 5% of American adults have ADHD.[17] Mostly, adults continue to struggle with inattention and impulsivity. In adulthood, inattention can cause missed appointments and deadlines on their jobs. Impulsivity can cause adults to walk off or be fired from their jobs for abandonment and can also lead to ongoing substance use. And hyperactivity can cause psychosocial difficulties, as peers and friends become annoyed with the person's ongoing movement and moodiness.

Throughout the lifespan of a person with ADHD, interpersonal relationships with peers can be strained. In the young, children's peers quickly recognize the hyperactivity and impulsivity that is commonly seen in children with ADHD. Impulsivity in young children usually presents as intrusive actions, like blurting out and interrupting others' conversations and games and hitting other children, and this can lead to children with ADHD being isolated on the playground and not invited to birthday parties, sleepovers, and other outings, for example.

SPOTLIGHT

The primary presenting symptom of ADHD for preschool-aged children is hyperactivity.

The primary presenting symptom of ADHD for early elementary-aged children is inattention.

"Reading" without comprehension is only saying words out loud.

The primary complaints for the adolescent are impulsivity and moodiness.

While certain symptoms are more likely to be seen in specific age groups, all symptoms of ADHD can present at any age.

CHAPTER FOUR

Treating ADHD

WHY DO WE TREAT ADHD?

The goal of treating ADHD symptoms is for your child who has ADHD to be less hyperactive, impulsive, and inattentive and to be successful in the classroom and life. Contrary to popular belief, success for a child with ADHD means more than making Honor Roll and staying seated in the class. Success for any child, but especially yours who has ADHD, means he or she is not missing time from school for fighting, is not moody and irritable, and is not having motor vehicle accidents. Success also means that he or she does as well as they possibly can in school, that they do not drop out of school, and that they do not use drugs.

It is important for you as a parent to understand that ADHD is a 24 hours-per-day, 7 days-per-week, 365 days-per-year disorder. This means that for every day your child awakens, there is a high likelihood that he or she will be hyperactive, impulsive, inattentive, or a combination of all three. For that reason, most children require treatment every day. You, like so many other parents, may feel medication holidays increase your child's appetite on the weekend or that they allow you to "have your child back," but this way of treatment can be disruptive to your child's overall functioning, and can lead to them getting hurt. For example, weekends and afternoons are the times that your child is least likely to have structure, which means they are more likely to do things that could cause themselves or others harm or danger. Some examples include running into the street to chase a wayward ball without looking both ways, leading to the child getting hit by a car. Or your child may forget they do not know how to swim and jump in the deep end of a body of water. Or your teenage driver may speed to make it through a yellow light only for it to change to red while they are in the intersection and this leads to them T-boning another car. These, like countless others, are examples of mishaps that occur at times when school is not in session, like after school, weekends, and holiday and seasonal breaks. These examples may also prove to be great reasons to continue medications even when there is no school and to skip the popular "medication holiday."

MEDICATION AS TREATMENT

ADHD is the most studied of all the mental health disorders that affect children. Psychotropic medications are also well studied and have been shown to be the most consistently effective treatment for ADHD. The National Institute of Mental Health (NIMH) conducted the most thorough study of treatments for

ADHD. The study, called the Multimodal Treatment Study of Children with ADHD (or the MTA), showed four things: 1) that methylphenidate (a commonly used stimulant medication for ADHD) is effective in treating the symptoms of ADHD when used either alone or with behavioral therapy; 2) that treatment which includes medication is more effective for the symptoms of ADHD (such as hyperactivity) than behavioral therapy alone; 3) that "in most cases, medication significantly reduces symptoms of ADHD, which makes it easier for children with ADHD to get along with their peers"; and 4) that the combination of behavioral treatment with medicine was useful in helping those who work with children with ADHD learn ways to change the behaviors that cause problems at school and at home.[19]

There are two major categories of medications that treat ADHD: psychostimulants ("stimulants"), which can further be broken down into two subclasses: amphetamines and methylphenidates, and non-stimulants. Both have proven over several decades to be highly effective treatments for ADHD. Specifically, amphetamines have been used for more than 70 years and methylphenidates have been used for more than 50 years to treat ADHD.[20]

PSYCHOSTIMULANT MEDICATIONS: AMPHETAMINES AND METHYLPHENIDATES

Psychostimulants are commonly called stimulants. There are two classes of stimulants: amphetamine and methylphenidate derivatives. Common amphetamine derivatives include the brand names Adderall and Vyvanse. Common methylphenidate derivatives include the brand names Ritalin, Concerta, QuilliChew, Quillivant, Focalin, Metadate, and Daytrana. It is important to note that the medications in each class are like siblings, which means that while they are different, they certainly are more alike. It is also like in comparing vehicles: GM makes several cars—GMC, Cadillac, Chevrolet, to name a few. The only difference between a Yukon, Escalade, and Suburban are the bells, whistles, and cost, and these are likened to the price placed on the medication and what your insurance may make affordable for you. (This is an important comparison, since all methylphenidates are like Ritalin, which families seem to shy away from.) You should also consider that what worked for one sibling may not work for another. Similarly, side effects seen in one medication may not be seen in another medication—even if it is in the same class. Regardless of the brand, both amphetamines and methylphenidates are safe when prescribed to healthy patients who are under medical supervision. Your child may need to try more than one medication before finding the one best for him or her. This is usual. However, if your child does not seem to be improving, symptoms should be reviewed and the diagnosis reconsidered.

When thinking about how a doctor chooses which medication to recommend, it is important for you to know that the practice of medicine is as dependent on science (the facts one learns in the classroom) as it is on art (the style with which one practices, which may change over time based on previous patients the doctor has treated). As such, several factors go into the decision of which medication to choose.

First, while it is widely understood and accepted that stimulant medications are the most consistently effective for treating ADHD, some parents just are not ready to start a stimulant in their child. Why do parents not want to start a stimulant? I am glad you asked. Here are a few reasons you may have avoided starting your child on stimulants:

- You may have heard or recall horrible stories about distant relatives or relatives of your friends "who took Ritalin back in the day and now only sit in the corner and rock." I cannot speak to what may have happened to that relative or friend, but it is highly unlikely that everything that is happening to them now is related exclusively to Ritalin.

- You do not want your child to be on "narcotics." To clarify, medically speaking, "narcotics" are opiate medications, which are typically used to treat pain. When the term "narcotics" is applied to stimulant medications, that usually is a legal, not medical, association. Not understanding these distinctions, parents sometimes wish to steer clear of anything related to the law.

- You fear your child will become addicted to the stimulant. Parents must understand that when children take medications as prescribed, they are much LESS likely to be impulsive. Less impulsivity means they will be less likely to engage in risky behaviors, like using drugs. Research has consistently shown this to be the case.

- You recall your own substance abuse history and wish to not have stimulant medications in the home as they may be a trigger for your relapse.

- You do not want your child to be labeled. Parents must know that labels are important to help educators and others who work with your child to know how to best treat them academically, socially, and emotionally.

- You feel guilty for treating your child's ADHD with medication. It's important to remember that ADHD is a medical condition, just as diabetes, hypertension (high blood pressure), and seizures are, and it should be treated with the same seriousness and consistency as any other medical illness would be.

- You want to punish your child until he or she focuses and gets better grades. Treating your child's ADHD with medication, praying, and using corporal punishment are not mutually exclusive. This means they can all be used at the same time. However, you want to make sure that your method of punishment is consistently effective. And related to corporal punishments, like whipping/whooping and spanking, you want to make sure you are careful to know, learn, and follow the laws that speak to corporal punishment in your governing area so that you do not violate any laws of physical or emotional abuse.

Once you have decided to use a stimulant, WHICH stimulant to choose first is the next major decision. There are several factors that must be considered before a medication can be started.

- Insurance: Insurance is one of the major determinants of which medication is chosen. A doctor may consider a certain medication for your child, but insurance may require a trial of one to two other medications before it will pay for the medication in question. Sometimes a prior authorization (PA), which asks the insurance to pay for a medication that is not considered one of their first-line medications, has to be submitted and approved before the insurance will pay for a non-preferred medication.

- FDA approval of medication based on age: Amphetamines are approved by the U.S. Food and Drug Administration (FDA) for children as young as three years old while methylphenidate medications are approved for children as young as six years old. Sometimes, however, your doctor may choose to use a medication in either class based on a variety of criteria, and that is ok.

- Age: Younger children have earlier bedtimes so they may need medications that have shorter durations of action (or are not effective for a long period of time). Contrarily, adolescents have more homework and extracurricular activities that require them to be awake for longer periods, and therefore benefit from longer-acting stimulant medications.

- Side effect profile: While all stimulants can cause irritability, some psychostimulants are known to cause increased irritability in children and adults alike. So choosing a medication based on side effect profile is always an appropriate consideration.

- Preparation of medication: Younger children may not be able to swallow a capsule and may do better with a chewable preparation, dissolvable preparation, liquid preparation, or even a topical preparation, like a patch.

- Doctor's past experiences: Doctors tend to prescribe medications they are familiar and/or comfortable with and that have been most effective in previous patients they have treated.

It is important for you to know that the strength of the medication will have to increase over time. The dose is calculated based on the weight of the child, so bigger children will need more medication and smaller children will need less. Most doctors will start at a lower strength and then will increase it over time; the speed with which they increase or the amount of time over which they do it will be based on the doctor's comfort level.

SIDE EFFECTS OF PSYCHOSTIMULANT MEDICATIONS

Psychostimulants are known for their very classic side effect profile. Some side effects are very common and should be expected. Other, more serious side effects, like those that affect the nervous and cardiac systems, are less common. No matter how insignificant you think a side effect is, you should report it to the physician. Some side effects can be reduced by decreasing medication dosage, splitting a dose, giving the medication at a different time of day, or ultimately changing medications.

Common side effects are just that: common.

Loss of Appetite: One of the most common side effects of stimulants is loss of appetite, which is seen in 50–60% of children who take stimulants.[21] Decreased appetite can be very real, and when it occurs, it can cause weight loss. One way to avoid this weight loss is to give your child breakfast before they take their morning medication and a snack before they take their afternoon, or "booster" dose, if the child takes one. Some parents avoid long-acting medications, as many of them tend to "peak" in effect just at lunch time, thus making appetite decrease at that time. One way to circumvent this mid-day decrease in appetite is to give multiple short-acting doses throughout the day, but you may find that dosing the medication several times per day may be inconvenient. You may not recognize it, but many children who take stimulants graze throughout the day and/or eat many snack foods, which means that their weight only takes very small decreases, if any at all. If you become concerned about your child's weight, you can also give meals high in caloric content and skip those items that may be considered diet foods. Offering your child a balanced, nutritional diet and allowing them to eat what they want and when they want, especially once a medication has been found to be effective when all others were not, may be a way to prevent weight loss. And finally, being flexible with the timing of meals is very important since medications may not stop working until 8 p.m. or 9 p.m., about the time when your young child is likely in bed.

Worsening Sleep: Another common side effect of stimulants is worsening sleep. A common co-occurring problem seen in children with ADHD is insomnia. Commonly, children with ADHD have problems initiating sleep. However, stimulant medications, as their name implies, make children awake and alert even at nighttime. One way to avoid this phenomenon is to give stimulants as far away from bedtime as possible, especially long-acting stimulants. It is important that you keep in mind that long-acting medications can last 6–12 hours and short-acting medications can last 2–6 hours and to plan accordingly when determining the type of medication to give and the time to give it.

Abdominal Pain: As many as 30–40% of children who take stimulants also complain of abdominal pain.[21] In large part this is because the children do not eat before taking the medications and their appetites are decreased after taking the medications. Eating before taking the medications can help reduce abdominal discomfort, much like it can help reduce the likelihood of weight loss. Some parents think of a child's eating before taking medication as providing a "coating" to the stomach lining. This may not be factual, but it may help with your understanding.

Headache: Headache is another side effect of stimulant medications, though it is not seen quite as commonly as decreased appetite and sleep disturbance. As with weight loss, headaches can often be linked to skipped meals, but they can occur regardless of the child's food intake with the medication. Sometimes changing to a different medication is the only thing that reduces headaches, as one would not typically suggest treating headaches with pain medications on a very frequent basis when they are a side effect of stimulant medications. At least, this will not be the recommendation before other medications have been tried.

Irritability: Irritability can be quite common in children with ADHD. As discussed above, because irritability and mood lability/instability can be common in ADHD, it is difficult to determine if the irritability is a side effect of the medication or if it is ongoing irritability that is a common symptom of ADHD in general. You may find that you have so much hope in medications and/or are looking for medications to take the blame for your child's symptoms that you blame the medication for the presenting irritability. It is not uncommon that when parents are asked to compare the child's symptoms before and after medication initiation, they respond, "Yeah… They were already having tantrums." Oftentimes, ongoing irritability, which can co-occur with tantrums, means that more medication is needed and not simply that a decrease or a change in medication needs to occur.

Behavioral Rebound: Behavioral rebound is a common phenomenon that many parents report. This is what happens when the child's daytime medication dose wears off and the result is an increase in irritability and hyperactivity in the mid-to-late-afternoon, or whenever the medication seems to no longer be working. Most often this occurs around the time that children would be expected to do homework, so you may initially think the child is just avoiding doing homework. Increasing the longer-acting daytime medication dose can be effective, but oftentimes adding an immediate-release medication in the afternoon is effective, too.

Serious side effects of stimulant medications include neurologic and cardiac side symptoms.

Serious side effects include those that affect the neurologic and cardiovascular systems or impact a child's life and/or safety. Neurologically, children who take stimulants are at an increased risk for seizures and tics.

Seizures: In theory, stimulants decrease the seizure threshold, meaning that your child might be more likely to have a seizure if taking a stimulant. Having a known seizure disorder, or epilepsy, is not necessarily a contraindication for taking psychostimulants. However, your child's neurologist should be closely involved in the management of the child's ADHD. In fact, many neurologists encourage their patients with seizures to have adequately controlled ADHD symptoms. This may likely be in part because several studies have shown that stimulants do not exacerbate well-controlled seizures.[22] (Of note, when considering children with autism spectrum disorder, know that about 30% of them also have seizures.[23] Also, a large percentage of children with autism spectrum disorder have ADHD. This means that children with autism are being treated with stimulants, and this can mean that there is an increased incidence of seizures when they take stimulants.) Again, working with the neurologist is key to making sure that children are psychologically and neurologically well when they are on stimulants and have seizures.

Tics: Tics, which are sudden, involuntary, uncontrollable movements, can be seen in children with ADHD. Tics can be verbal, motor, or both. Motor tics are short-lasting, sudden movements. Examples of motor tics can be eye blinking, grimacing, jerking or banging the head, shrugging shoulders, or finger movements. Examples of vocal tics can be coughing, grunting, sniffing, snorting, humming, barking, spitting, and repeating a sound or phrase. (Of note, obscene or offensive verbalizations are extremely rare.) Tics usually are not permanent and usually subside once the inciting medication is decreased or discontinued.

From a cardiovascular, or heart, standpoint, psychostimulants have been proven to not increase the risk of death from heart disease. In a study involving 1.2 million children and young adults, it was found that cardiac problems were no more common among children using a stimulant than in those not taking one. Among children, heart attack, stroke, or sudden death were rare, affecting little more than three in every 100,000 children per year in the study.[24] Some other studies have shown that in cases where there are sudden deaths related to a cardiac issue, underlying, undiagnosed cardiac history played a role.

Initially, the American Heart Association suggested that children being evaluated for ADHD have an electrocardiogram (EKG/ECG) but the leading pediatric group, the American Academy of Pediatrics (AAP), cited that the rarity or infrequency with which pediatric cardiac deaths occur does not necessitate a need for EKGs in all children starting stimulants. According to AAP analysis, cardiac deaths occur in about two children for every million taking ADHD medications, and this is fewer than the eight to sixty-two sudden deaths per million that occur in the general pediatric population.[24] The most important factor in assessing cardiac risk is taking a thorough history and examination. This should include asking about past medical history, including congenital heart disease, fainting spells, heart palpitations, and family history, including sudden and unexpected death in persons younger than 35 years old. One simple question, "Has your child ever seen a cardiologist, or heart doctor?" as well as follow-up questions regarding the reason for the visit, the result of the visit, restrictions or limitations, and future follow-up appointments can be very telling. It is also particularly helpful to know if a child has had any cardiac surgeries.

Like heart disease and sudden deaths, tachycardia (increased heart rate) is not seen as often as originally thought in children or adults, further making stimulant medications an option for the treatment of ADHD.[24]

In summary, the risk of neurological and cardiovascular side effects related to stimulant medications is low. If your child has a personal or family history of neurologic and/or cardiovascular symptoms, he or she should be followed closely by their primary care doctor, neurologist and/or cardiologist, and psychiatrist to ensure best prognosis.

Rare side effects of stimulants occur…rarely.

Hallucinations: Rare or serious side effects include those that can cause psychosis. Hallucinations related to stimulants are usually visual or tactile. Visual hallucinations are those that are seen. Tactile hallucinations are those that cause a person to feel as if something is touching their skin. Children who experience hallucinations often report seeing bugs crawling in front of them or feeling bugs crawling on them when they take stimulants. Hallucinations can be scary but usually are not permanent. They usually subside when the medication is changed.

Suspiciousness: Parents sometimes report that their children seem more suspicious when taking stimulant medications. Again, this is very rare and subsides once the medication is discontinued.

Depression: Depression is infrequently seen with stimulant medications. Some parents note that their children are "too focused" and that they only seem to look into space. Often, changing the medications means that their mood resumes to one more typical of what the child had prior to beginning medications.

Mania: Rarely, stimulants can cause a child to "switch" into a manic-like episode. These symptoms often include decreased need for sleep, increased goal-directed activity, racing thoughts, pressured speech, and inflated thoughts of self. Note that these symptoms are not truly indicative of a manic episode since a manic episode must occur without the influence of any substance, prescribed or otherwise.

Suicidal Thoughts: Some families report suicidal thoughts in their children who take stimulant medications. However, it is worth noting that this is very rare. The benefits of treating ADHD still outweigh the small risk that a child will hurt himself or herself. Parents should closely monitor their child for any changes in mood, interest, or activity and should report those to the psychiatrist, take the child to the closest emergency department, or call 911 if safety is a concern.

Other Parental Concerns about Psychostimulant Medications:

You may have other worries, like about things such as drug addiction, changes in personality, or your child being like a distant relative who took medications in the 1990s and now "just isn't right" or "sits in a corner and rocks."

Substance Use: Regarding substance use, children whose ADHD is treated and is well-controlled are less impulsive and, therefore, are less likely to engage in risky behaviors, like substance use, reckless driving, and sexual promiscuity. Repeatedly, it has been studied and found that treating a child's ADHD at a younger age decreases the likelihood that they will use illicit drugs in the future. You should also know that, compared to prescribed stimulant medications, methamphetamine ("meth") and cocaine are both illicit drugs that have very powerful addictive potential and can quickly cause addiction and physical dependence, which causes uncomfortable, sometimes dangerous consequences. Specifically, crack cocaine, the "rock" form of cocaine, reaches the brain faster than other methods of cocaine because it is smoked. This can cause addiction more quickly than other forms of cocaine and each use can lead to a fatal overdose. And to be clear, methamphetamine is not the same as methylphenidate or amphetamine, which are both commonly prescribed to children and adults for ADHD.

The "Zombie" Child: Many parents often comment that they "want to keep the child's personality" or they do not want their child to be a "zombie." You should be prepared for your child to be a little different, but only from the perspective that he or she will now be able to complete tasks and remain normoactive. A child whose ADHD is treated will be able to complete tasks the way they were assigned or requested and they will not be as hyperactive and impulsive. For example, parents can expect that when told to "go in the kitchen, get an orange, cut it in fourths and put a fourth of the orange on a red plate," the child will neither go in the kitchen and just look around, nor will they bring a fourth of a red apple on an orange plate. So yes! They will be different, but in a way that you will welcome and be excited about. However, if you find that your child only "stares into space" or does not interact as much as he or she did in the past, be sure to mention this to the child's doctor. Adjustments in or changes to medications can always be considered.

Changing Interests: Some parents have concerns about their children not maintaining their interests and personality. The goal for children taking stimulant medications is for them to be focused and have normal activity. They should maintain their interests, goals, and play despite being on medications. They just may be able to do it quietly, without getting distracted, and until it is completed. If you find that you do not like how quiet, emotionless, or void of hyperactivity your child is, you need to mention it to your child's doctor. Simple medication adjustments or changing the medication altogether can lessen these effects.

Short Stature: Some parents worry that their children's growth will be stunted when they take stimulant medications. Several studies have addressed that issue. Some have postulated that ADHD itself is responsible for the less than one-inch reduction in growth compared to peers who do not take ADHD medications. Some others have postulated that the decrease in nutrients and calories that children with ADHD consume because of decreased appetite is to blame. Others believe that maybe stimulant medications are to blame for the decrease in height. And finally, some others have thought that the combination of ADHD, stimulant medications, and decreased caloric intake are all to blame for the very insignificant decrease in height. The truth, in summary, is this: there is no noticeable height difference in children who take stimulants compared to children who do not take stimulants.[25] However, as with all other parental concerns, worries about your child's height and/or growth should be presented to the psychiatrist and then medication adjustments or changes can be made at that time.

In summary, even though common, serious, rare, or concerning side effects can occur, a physician should always address them in simple, honest, and empathetic terms. Medication adjustments can always be made. And while the emphasis continues to be on the child getting better, sometimes you may not be able to handle the side effects, or more often, the guilt you feel for giving your child medications, and you will discontinue them. And unless other agencies are involved that have medical decision-making privileges for your child, that is always your right as the parent.

NON-STIMULANT MEDICATIONS

Some parents do not like the side effect profile of stimulants or even the idea of their child taking a stimulant, but they may agree to try a non-stimulant medication for ADHD symptoms. There are four non-stimulant medications that are used for ADHD: Strattera (atomoxetine), Tenex and Intuniv (short and long-acting guanfacine, respectively), and Kapvay (clonidine). Tenex, the short-acting form of guanfacine, is the only non-stimulant medication that is not FDA-approved for the treatment of ADHD. Like stimulant medications, several factors are considered when determining which non-stimulant medication your child's doctor may choose.

- Insurance: Most non-stimulant medications are covered by insurance. However, there may be a limit on the number of pills/tablets that can be dispensed (given to the patient each month).

- FDA approval: All non-stimulants, except Tenex, are FDA-approved to treat ADHD.

- Age: Many doctors choose non-stimulant medications over stimulants when the patient is very young. This is often the doctor's preference and does not mean that the child cannot take and benefit from a stimulant.

- Side effect profile: The non-stimulants can cause lowered blood pressure, so that is something to consider.

- Preparation of medication: Non-stimulants do not have as many preparations as stimulants. Strattera is a capsule, guanfacine as Intuniv is a long-acting tablet and as Tenex is a short-acting tablet, and clonidine is a tablet.

- Parent comfort: Some parents just do not like the idea of giving "strong, mind-altering" medications to young children, so they prefer non-stimulants for that reason.

- Doctor's past experiences: Again, doctors tend to prescribe medications they are familiar and/or comfortable with and have had the most positive effect with.

Non-Stimulant Medications: Strattera

Strattera is a norepinephrine reuptake inhibitor, is not a controlled substance (or what some parents would call a "narcotic"), and has no potential for abuse, which excites most parents. Strattera is active for 24 hours, which allows for it to be given at night. This may be necessary in some cases since the medication can cause sedation. Unlike stimulants, which are active only on the days the child takes them and leave the body within 2-14 hours, depending on the medication, Strattera stays at a baseline level (called steady state) all the time, which means that you will not notice your child's symptoms increasing and decreasing throughout the day. Reaching this baseline level may take time; sometimes you may not notice maximum benefit and decrease in symptoms until four to six weeks. And because this baseline level must be maintained, Strattera should be taken daily; otherwise, you may always be starting over in an attempt to reach the baseline level again. This makes Strattera less-than-ideal for patients whose parents wish to give medication holidays, or for patients who live between two homes where one parent or guardian does not give medication on weekends, for example.

Side Effects of Non-Stimulant Medications: Strattera

Strattera has some potential side effects. Here are a few:

- Black Box Warning: There is a Black Box Warning that advises against suicidal thoughts or behaviors in children and adolescents. These were only seen in a very small number of cases when studied, but as with any other risks, if your child is affected, it is a high percentage to you. If present, these thoughts usually occur in the first couple weeks of treatment. Discontinuing the medication makes any thoughts of suicide related to the medication subside.

- Abdominal side effects: As with stimulant medications, Strattera can cause nausea, decreased appetite, and weight loss. Also, as with stimulant medications, giving the medication with food is helpful in decreasing these symptoms.

- Drowsiness: All non-stimulants can cause drowsiness. To avoid this, some parents have found that giving these medications at night helps to decrease daytime sedation. Specifically, since Strattera claims to last 24 hours, giving it at night should mean that it will still work throughout the next day. Note that giving stimulants at nighttime is not suggested because the child is less likely to sleep at night.

- Liver damage: Severe liver damage has been associated with Strattera; however, this is a very rare finding. Liver function tests should not be ordered for every patient taking Strattera, but only for the patient who has known or suspected liver damage. Signs of liver damage could include pruritus (itching), yellowing of the skin or eyes, right upper abdominal pain, and unexplained "flu-like" symptoms.

- Cardiovascular risks: Despite Strattera not affecting the body physiologically in the same way that stimulants can, Strattera can still cause increases in pulse and blood pressure. As with stimulants, these changes are extremely rare and often subside when the medication is discontinued.[26]

Non-Stimulant Medications: Long-Acting Guanfacine

Long-acting guanfacine (Intuniv), by design, is an anti-hypertensive medication in the alpha agonist class of medications. (It treats high blood pressure.) Intuniv has been used to treat children with ADHD who have tics, sleep problems, and/or aggression, and it has FDA approval. It is not a controlled substance or "narcotic" and does not have potential for abuse, which is comforting to many parents. One of its few drawbacks is that it is a pill that cannot be crushed, chewed, or in any way destroyed; it must be swallowed whole. This can be problematic for very young children, who tend to be the most likely population to take the medication. It is a blood pressure medication so in theory it can lower blood pressure and/or pulse.

Of note, the short-acting form of guanfacine, Tenex, does not have FDA approval for the treatment of ADHD. However, it functions the same as Intuniv, the longer-acting form of the medication, except for needing to be dosed more frequently throughout the day than Intuniv. Despite the lack of FDA approval for the treatment of ADHD, many doctors will prescribe it "off-label."

Side Effects of Non-Stimulant Medications: Guanfacine

Among the most common side effects of guanfacine are drowsiness and fatigue. Sleepiness is usually more prominent at the beginning of treatment with long-acting guanfacine but that seems to lessen as time passes. Because guanfacine is an alpha agonist, a class of medications that lower blood pressure, it can lower your child's blood pressure. (However this is not a common finding.) Appetite suppression is a less typical side effect, so it may be a good choice for children who experienced appetite suppression or lost weight when taking a stimulant, or whose parents have concerns about their weight. It can also cause dry mouth, constipation, and abdominal pain. One significant fact about using guanfacine is that three to four weeks may pass before you see any decrease in symptoms.

Non-Stimulant Medications: Long-Acting Clonidine

Long-acting clonidine (Kapvay) is also FDA-approved for the treatment of ADHD. Kapvay is a long-acting alpha agonist, which means it can also lower blood pressure. It is not a controlled substance or "narcotic" and does not have potential for abuse. It can be taken twice a day while long-acting guanfacine is taken once daily. Kapvay and Intuniv can be used alone or in combination with a stimulant; this can be useful when the stimulant alone is not effective at controlling all the symptoms of ADHD or if your child is taking the maximum strength of a preferred stimulant based on weight but still has some residual symptoms of ADHD. Of note, the shorter-acting alpha agonist (clonidine, which is branded as Catapres) is not FDA-approved for the treatment of ADHD. It can be used as adjunctive medication, or if FDA-approved medications are not helpful.

Side Effects of Non-Stimulant Medications: Clonidine

Besides being a medication used to treat high blood pressure, clonidine can cause significant sedation. Many doctors prescribe it for its sedating properties in children with ADHD who cannot sleep.

ANTIDEPRESSANTS THAT TREAT ADHD

Bupropion (Wellbutrin) is an antidepressant and is also used for smoking cessation and weight loss. It has not been extensively studied as a treatment for ADHD so it does not have FDA approval for this diagnosis. Some research has shown that it may be helpful in reducing ADHD symptoms in children, but with less effect than the stimulants or atomoxetine (Strattera). However, it may be a third-line choice for ADHD, especially for someone with comorbid ADHD and depression. (Of note, bupropion is not approved for the treatment of depression in children under 18 years old.)

Side Effects of Bupropion

Mostly, the side effects of bupropion are usually minimal. Side effects can include irritability, decreased appetite, insomnia, and a worsening of existing tics. It is important to note that at higher doses, bupropion can lower the seizure threshold, making some people more likely to have a seizure. Bupropion is not contraindicated (meaning there is no rule that it should not be used) in people with a known seizure disorder, but it should be used cautiously in people who have seizures. Contrarily, bupropion is contraindicated in people with bulimia because they can have abnormal electrolytes due to purging (self-induced vomiting or using laxatives or other medications to induce stooling), which can lower the seizure threshold before the medication is introduced. Bupropion can also cause hallucinations.

BEHAVIOR MODIFICATION AS TREATMENT

Hands down, the best treatment for ADHD is a combination of medication and therapy. Even alone, behavioral therapy is another very important option for the treatment of ADHD but sometimes it is not enough. Most professionals recommend children engage in behavioral therapy as soon as they receive a diagnosis of ADHD, regardless of their age. Some even go further and recommend that preschool age children (less than six years old) start behavioral therapy before starting medications. The decision to start therapy with or without medication is best determined on a case-by-case basis as some children are too hyperactive, inattentive, and/or impulsive to engage in and benefit from behavioral therapy in a meaningful way without medication.

Behavioral therapy, unlike psychotherapy or play therapy, focuses on changing actions (behaviors), not emotions. In behavioral therapy children learn how to turn unwanted, disruptive energy into positive thoughts and actions.

Three types of therapies are generally considered for children with ADHD: parent training, child-focused treatment, and school-based interventions.

- Parent Training helps parents learn about ADHD and ways to manage ADHD behaviors.

- Child-Focused Treatment helps children and teens with ADHD learn to develop social, academic, and problem-solving skills.

- School-Based Interventions help teachers meet children's educational needs by teaching them skills to manage the children's ADHD behaviors in the classroom (such as rewards, consequences, and daily report cards sent to parents).[19]

Therapy: Behavioral Parent Training (BPT)

In this book, we will focus on parent training. In parent training, parents, caregivers, and sometimes even teachers have a key leading role. Behavioral therapists refer to this type of therapy as behavioral management training for parents, parent behavior training, and behavioral parent training (BPT); we will use the latter term for discussion here.

Many parents are offended at the suggestion of behavioral parent training because of the name, which they report suggests that they are not good parents or are not parenting "right." Often they exclaim "I am a good parent! I parented my other kids and they were just fine!" The truth of the matter is that parents have often been great at parenting and the parenting techniques they used with their other children were effective. However, it is likely those other children did not have ADHD and, therefore, the unique parenting skills needed for parenting a child with ADHD were not needed when parenting those children who did not have it.

Dysfunctional and inconsistent parenting is usually a key focus of behavior management interventions. Parents of children with ADHD tend to show more negative and ineffective parenting (e.g., power assertive, punitive, inconsistent) and less positive or warm parenting relative to parents of children without ADHD. Family conflict tends to be high in homes where a child with ADHD lives. Therapy such as behavioral parent training directly targets these parenting styles in order to improve the child's behaviors and family relationships, and to reduce overall family conflict and stress.

The theoretical basis of behavioral parent training is contingency theory and social learning theory. In contingency theory, a child's behavior can be increased by giving a rewarding stimulus (i.e., positive reinforcement) or by removing an aversive stimulus (i.e., negative reinforcement). Conversely, behavior can be decreased by following it with an aversive stimulus (i.e., extinction). Simply put, obtaining a reward for doing something good likely means that a child will do it again, and getting punished after doing something not good likely means the child will not do it again. With consistent use of contingency management over time, the child's behavior can be shaped to achieve desired goals. (Some common goals parents have for their children with ADHD are that they will make their beds, attend to homework, and have decreased frequency of tantrums.)

In addition to contingency theory, behavior management treatment is also grounded in social learning theory, which considers contingency theory principles alongside other factors including modeling and imitation of observed behaviors (e.g., parent behaviors) as well as cognitive factors (e.g., parental appraisals and attributions of child behavior.)

The first step in designing a behavior management intervention involves gathering information about the child's behaviors, what things cause them, and what happens after they end. This process is called functional behavior analysis. Part of this analysis includes identifying target areas to increase, called positive behaviors, and target areas to decrease, called negative behaviors. The next step is to identify the events in the child's environment occurring immediately before and after the behavior. These events are called antecedents and consequences, respectively. Behaviors, their antecedents, and consequences are defined so that they are objective and measurable. Identifying these events in the environment helps to determine the reason for the behavior. For example, some children are seeking to avoid attending school, others to do homework, and still others are attempting to get attention. (Notice that either avoiding a task or gaining something, like their parents' attention, can be the reason for the behavior.) The behaviors usually represent areas of functional impairment impacting the child in his or her everyday life. Often, these symptoms are consistent with classic ADHD symptoms. After the analysis, a behavior plan can be developed that changes the antecedents and consequences which have been maintaining the target behavior, thereby modifying the likelihood of the behavior in the desired direction (e.g., increases positive behavior and reduces negative behavior).[27]

Conducting a functional behavior analysis is only one part of beginning to understand and change children's behaviors. Another key component of behavior modification is changing negative parent-child interaction patterns, referred to as the "coercive process," and it works both ways. Parents and children control the others' actions by negative reinforcement (removing aversive stimuli). One example is when a parent asks a child to complete a task. When the child does not, the parent responds in a negative way, the child responds similarly, and a cycle of alternating noncompliance and anger repeats itself and worsens in severity and emotional involvement as time goes on until either the parent or child gives in. This ends the cycle for that moment but also reinforces the negative escalated behaviors that started the cycle. The cycle reinforces the functional impairments and related conduct problems seen in children with ADHD. This explains how the coercive parent-child interaction cycle predicts poor educational outcomes, peer relations, social skills, and aggressive behavior. Furthermore, parenting styles associated with the coercive cycle mediate the effects of contextual risk factors such as stress, parental depression, and social disadvantage on child behavior problems. Behavior management training directly targets these dysfunctional parenting practices by teaching families how to modify antecedents and consequences to reduce the likelihood of the coercive process and improve child behaviors and family relationships.

It is known that behavioral approaches are needed in children with ADHD. Studies have shown that ADHD is associated with neural-based motivational systems that do not respond to the kinds of contingencies that teachers and parents typically use. Specifically, compared to children without ADHD, children with ADHD are less responsive to inconsistent, delayed, and weak reinforcement, and to cues of punishment or non-reward. Fundamental to behavior management interventions is a focus on modifying parent- and teacher-delivered rewards and consequences. These practices, together with the additional external structure provided by behavioral interventions, can also help address the executive weaknesses that are a part of ADHD.

As far as treatment delivery, behavioral parent training includes eight to twelve group and/or individual sessions focused on three main objectives:

1. Providing psychoeducation about ADHD and the behavioral framework for treatment.

2. Teaching effective parenting skills for improving desired behavior and decreasing problem behavior through altering antecedents and consequences.

3. Practicing/troubleshooting effective implementation of skills learned.

Each session has a teaching portion, when you learn new information, and an interactive portion, when you can discuss the implementation of parenting skills you previously learned. The most important part of the "homework" is applying newly learned skills at home and then monitoring the child's behavior. This will serve as the basis for discussion and troubleshooting at each visit.

Families who are able to attend treatment sessions regularly and consistently implement the interventions at home tend to have the most favorable outcomes. Families with sufficient resources, like transportation, time available to attend sessions, childcare for siblings, and financial/health care resources, are more likely to follow through more consistently. Two-parent families, those with social support, and those with low levels of parental stress and psychopathology (e.g., ADHD, depression) tend to have more favorable outcomes.[27] Parents' engagement in behavioral parent training can be increased when parents have positive expectations for results and believe the child can change. The likelihood of early termination can be reduced by including a portion of behavioral parent therapy that focuses on the child. This finding suggests that including the child in treatment may have a positive effect on parents' motivation for treatment. The severity of the child's symptoms and impairments can certainly influence outcomes, as children with moderate (rather than severe) symptoms seem to have more benefits of the combined intervention on homework problems. On the contrary, behavioral interventions appear to be equally effective for those with or without co-occurring oppositional or conduct problems and/or comorbid anxiety and both boys and girls through the school-age range (age 6 to 12 years) respond well to behavioral intervention. Lastly, race and ethnicity are not significant variables, as behavioral interventions tend to be successful across races and ethnicities, but there may need to be some changes to account for cultural differences.

So, does therapy work? Behavioral interventions are often used along with medication for optimal effects. In the large-scale, multi-site MTA study, which compared separate and combined effects of behavioral interventions and stimulant medication, combined treatment showed increasing benefit on parent and teacher behavior ratings.[19]

As far as effectiveness, traditional behavioral parent training may not be the best option for parents who cannot commit to keeping the demands outlined in the therapy, including time and effort to attend weekly sessions and implement behavioral plans between sessions at home. Also, parents with significant psychopathology (such as anger management problems, ADHD, depression, and substance use), limited cognitive capacity, or those in highly conflicted marital/partner relationships may be unlikely to participate in treatment. Child symptom severity is an important consideration and severe levels of ADHD symptoms and impairment often dictate combined treatment approaches. In general, optimal sequencing and integration of behavior management and medication require considering the dose or intensity of each treatment. Based on recent studies of varying doses/intensities of behavioral and medication treatments, fewer benefits of combined treatments are observed when the dosage of either treatment is high. Therefore, the optimal dose needed for medication is less when behavioral interventions are in place and the combination of low doses of each intervention is equivalent to a high dose of either treatment alone. Given the interactive effects of behavioral interventions and medication, it is imperative that treatment providers closely collaborate to optimize outcomes.[27]

Therapy: Child-Focused Treatment

Child-focused treatment helps children and teens with ADHD learn to develop social, academic, and problem-solving skills.

Behavioral parent training has also been combined with child treatments including behavioral peer interventions and child skills training. These treatments generally focus on improving social interactions and/or study/organizational skills. One example is the Child Life and Attention Skills Program (CLAS). CLAS uses behavioral parent training that has been adapted for inattention-related target behaviors and problems with executive functioning through rehabilitative psychology techniques. The goal of CLAS is to help children with inattention learn skills for independence, like organizational skills and daily living skills, and social skills, like conversation and friendship-making. CLAS includes parents, teachers, and children in the intervention. In CLAS, parents meet weekly to learn ways to help their child manage their inattention symptoms at home, and ways to best work with their child's teacher. Children also attend weekly groups where they learn skills and strategies to learn social and organizational skills needed in everyday life. Teachers receive training on how to best help the child with ADHD manage their symptoms throughout the day. Teachers complete a daily report card and meet with the child and/or his parents up to four times to monitor the child's progress and discuss possible changes to their behavioral goals.[27]

Therapy: School-Based Interventions

School-based interventions such as rewards, consequences, and daily report cards sent to parents help teachers meet children's educational needs by teaching them skills to manage the children's ADHD behaviors in the classroom. Many behavioral training therapy programs add school-based interventions, such as a Daily Report Card (DRC) system. Daily report cards are individually designed for each child and include target problem behaviors in academic and/or social domains displayed in the classroom. (Often the academic struggles are related to inattention.) Teachers rate the child daily based on target behaviors, and parents give the child a home-based reward, all based on the Daily Report Card, which the teacher sends each day. This system allows immediate feedback and rewards for the child and allows the parent and teacher to have ongoing communication, which ultimately will lead to the child's attention, behaviors, and social skills improving.

COMPLEMENTARY OPTIONS TO TREATMENT

You may be wondering about alternatives to medication to treat your child's ADHD, and you are not alone. Most parents inquire about alternatives even if they choose a prescription medication instead. The truth is there are options. And these options can be beneficial in the overall health of your child. However, none of these options have proven to be consistently effective in adequately controlling a child's symptoms of hyperactivity, impulsivity, or inattention. Here are some of the more commonly considered alternative treatments:

Complementary Treatment Options: Diet

Many parents suspect and even report noticing that their children are less hyperactive when certain items are removed from their diets.

One item is sugar. Many parents feel that sugar, whether in food or drinks, increases their child's hyperactivity. However, despite what parents have noticed, children who meet criteria for ADHD, and not simply those who are hyperactive, will not show any substantial changes in behavior when sugar is removed from the diet. It is worth noting that there may be some benefits of removing sugar from the diet, like decreasing the child's risk for obesity, a serious chronic medical condition in the United States that can begin in childhood and, over time, cause many other significant medical problems, like diabetes and cardiovascular disease. Another benefit of decreasing sugar intake in children is that the risk for tooth decay decreases, as there is a direct link between sugar and cavities. (Sugar molecules combine with oral bacteria and saliva, and these lead to plaque on the teeth, which can dissolve enamel and lead to cavities.) In short, there is no evidence that a diet without sugar will help the symptoms of ADHD, but reducing sugar can have other health benefits.

Other parents have found that removing artificial food coloring and additives from the diet has been effective in controlling hyperactivity. This has not been substantiated in large trials. Additionally, recall that not everyone who has ADHD has hyperactivity, so for those without hyperactivity, this would not be a viable treatment option. In short, there is no evidence that a diet without additives will consistently decrease the symptoms of ADHD.

Common allergens have been listed by some as a contributor for children to lose focus and be hyperactive. Some suggest that some of the leading culprits are gluten, wheat, corn, and soy and some go even further to suggest that children be screened for food allergies as a part of the initial assessment for ADHD. While controlling food and environmental allergies can be beneficial for the child's safety, quality of life, and overall well-being, there is not necessarily a need to rule them out prior to initiating treatment for ADHD. However, you should certainly work with your child's primary doctor to design a plan to best address those concerns. But as for allergens, there is no evidence that allergens significantly contribute to the presenting symptoms in a child with ADHD.

Complementary Treatment Options: Supplements

Supplements are an example of how too much of a good thing could be bad for you.

If a child has deficiencies in iron, zinc, or magnesium, for example, making sure the child has a balanced diet is the first treatment, then supplementing can be beneficial. Parents should be mindful that megavitamins, or large doses of vitamins, can be harmful to the liver. However, any benefits to ADHD symptoms are minimal and have not been confirmed by research. There is no evidence to suggest that supplements are sufficient to consistently reduce symptoms of ADHD.

Omega-3 fatty acid, commonly referred to as "fish oil," has been considered as a treatment for ADHD. One trial studied 92 children between 6 and 18 years old who had ADHD. Initially, participants' blood levels of EPA (eicosapentaenoic acid, a polyunsaturated fatty acid commonly found in fish) were measured. The children were then either given omega-3 fatty acid EPA or a placebo, a substance that has no therapeutic effect, used as a control in testing new drugs. The study revealed that "children with low EPA levels showed improvement in their abilities to focus and maintain attention. However, the children who had normal or high levels of EPA did not have any improvement in their ADHD symptoms, and some displayed an increase in impulsivity."[28] These results lead to the thought that omega-3 supplements worked only to replenish a lack of the nutrient omega-3 and that it could play a role in children who have a deficiency of the nutrient. However, including fish in the diet multiple times per week could have the same effect. In fact, "currently, the American Heart Association recommends two servings a week of fatty fish, such as salmon, mackerel, herring, lake trout, sardines, and albacore tuna." This is thought to be sufficient to maintain adequate levels of EPA such that supplementation is not necessary.[29] Some think that EPA deficiency is more common among children with ADHD in countries with less fish consumption, such as North America and many countries in Europe, and that fish oil supplementation could therefore have more widespread benefits. However, these theories have not been studied on a large scale and at this time have not been shown to be consistently effective for a majority of children.[28]

Complementary Treatment Options: Herbs

Herbs have calming qualities and they may play a role in memory and thinking. However, because herb products are not regulated, you cannot be assured of the purity (that it actually is what you think it is), safety (that it will not cause your child harm), or potential for toxicity (the ability to cause harm) that each one has.

Some examples of herbs that can be used to improve focus, attention, and/or memory include: French Maritime pine bark extract, which is a plant-based material that may increase visual-motor coordination and reduce hyperactivity and inattentiveness; ginseng, which is a Chinese herb that may alleviate hyperactivity and inattentiveness; nindong, which is also a Chinese medicine that may help to reduce some ADHD symptoms;[30] bacopa, which might reduce restlessness and improve self-control; valerian, which helps to sustain attention and reduce impulsivity and/or hyperactivity; ginkgo biloba, which is one of the more commonly known agents for increasing mental sharpness and improving memory; and blue-green algae, which is used to improve memory.

Though herbal medicines exist and are effective in some instances, you should know that studies that review these medications are mixed and do not consistently show effects on symptoms of ADHD. More large-scale research is needed to know if the herbal medications are truly safe and effective and at what strength they are effective. Research is also needed to know which prescribed medications and over-the-counter medications should be avoided when taking herbal medications. You should also understand that very few treatments, including herbal ones, are without side effects. (This is important because many parents choose herbal options to avoid side effects of the more traditional, prescribed medications that are used to treat ADHD.) For example, valerian can cause headaches. Blue-green algae can cause stomach upset, weakness, numbness, and tingling. Ginkgo biloba can cause headaches, dizziness, palpitations, stomach upset and skin rashes and should not be used in children with clotting problems.

Complementary Treatment Options: Homeopathy

Homeopathy uses combinations of plant, animal, or mineral extracts. No studies have shown that homeopathy is effective in treating ADHD. It should still be considered "experimental."

Complementary Treatment Options: Neurofeedback/Biofeedback

Neurofeedback, which is sometimes called feedback or electroencephalographic (EEG) biofeedback, is a treatment option for ADHD that is based on altering the speed of the electrical wave activity that the brain emits. It is based on the fact that an EEG has shown that the brain has several brain frequencies (or speeds) depending on if we are awake or asleep. These are called

- alpha (medium) waves, which are seen when a person is in a relaxed state and is not actively thinking or interacting with one's environment.

- beta (fast) waves, which are present when a person is interacting with the surrounding environment and is concentrating, thinking, or solving problems.

- theta (slow) waves, which are often seen during times of drowsiness, daydreaming or during light sleep, but can also occur during thoughtless, restless overactivity.

- delta waves, which are seen during deep sleep.

According to Children and Adults with Attention-Deficit/Hyperactivity Disorder (CHADD), who wrote an article on EEG feedback, "Many children with ADHD have slow arousal levels in the frontal parts of the brain with an excess of theta waves and a deficit of beta waves. This is the basis for neurofeedback/biofeedback, which is based on the thought that the brain can be trained to increase the levels of arousal by increasing beta waves and decreasing theta waves, which should lead to a reduction in ADHD symptoms."[31]

Neurofeedback treatment involves placing electrodes on a person's head to monitor brain activity. He or she is then given feedback with simple or complex cues, like an audible beep or a video game character moving in the correct direction when the desired brainwave frequency is reached. Supporters of neurofeedback believe that when the patient learns how to increase these arousal levels, attention will improve and hyperactive/impulsive behavior will decrease.

As far as effectiveness, there are five levels of grading of evidence used by the American Psychological Association that speak to how effective neurofeedback is as a treatment for ADHD. These levels are discussed here. Level 1 is "not empirically supported" and Level 5 is "efficacious and specific." CHADD's Professional Advisory Board reviewed several articles over 25 years and determined that Level 2 ("possibly efficacious") best reflects what published articles report. Level 2 assignment means that it "has shown to have a significant impact in at least one study, but the study lacked a randomized assignment between controls." (Note that randomized controls are considered the gold standard for determining effectiveness of medications and other treatments.)[31]

When determining if any treatment is appropriate for your child or you, it is necessary to review risks and benefits. Neurofeedback has little efficacy. Yet it is expensive because it requires a trained operator and 40 or more sessions that are typically administered by psychologists at their usual professional rate. Home kits exist but it is difficult to determine the consistency with which they are given, and this could mean that their results may be different from those obtained in a clinical or research setting.

Neurofeedback continues to create much interest and attention as a treatment for ADHD from both researchers and patients. However, to-date research still does not support claims about its efficacy. Based on the known evidence and cost, you should use caution when considering neurofeedback as an intervention for treating your child's ADHD.

THE IMPORTANCE OF ORGANIZATION AND STRUCTURE

Children, in general, do best when they have structure. They need to know the rules of the game of life if they are to succeed. This means they must know the rules of the home and the rules must be kept consistently.

Specifically, children with ADHD function better when they have consistency, organization, and structure. Having a specific place for all their items means they will know where they are when they are dressing, and this will mean mornings are much better. It will mean that car keys will always be in the same place so they will not be late to school or appointments. And it will mean that their homework will be in the bookbag and their bookbag in the car so they can turn it in when they get to school.

Each family should learn what organization system works for them and be diligent about maintaining that organization.

SPOTLIGHT

Medications that treat ADHD can be long-acting or short-acting. They come in capsules, some of which can be opened and the contents sprinkled onto food or in beverages, or as tablets. Some medications are chewable, and these can be long-acting or short-acting. They can be dissolvable. They can be liquid and be long-acting or short-acting. They can be a patch. For a comprehensive list of medications with true-to-size pictures, please see Cohen Children's Medical Center ADHD Medication Guide.[20]

The active ingredient in Ritalin, methylphenidate, is the same as in all other medications in its class.

Research continues to prove that children with ADHD are much less likely to abuse substances if their ADHD is treated.

Doctors often "start low and go slow" when prescribing medications. This means medications are typically started at lower doses and they will need to be increased over time.

Medication strength (milligrams=mg) can be likened to clothing sizes: get the size (strength) you need and can safely wear (tolerate and be positively affected by).

Consider that your child is not making a curtain call once in bed (an attempt to avoid going to bed or sleep) and that they are actually hungry if they consistently report being hungry between 8 p.m. and 9 p.m.

Obscene or offensive verbalizations, or tics, are extremely rare.

Heart attack, stroke, or sudden death are very rare complications of stimulants.

Because of the infrequency of pediatric cardiac deaths, an EKG is not necessary before starting stimulants.

The most important factor in assessing cardiac risk is taking very thorough personal and family histories and a thorough examination of the patient.

Auditory hallucinations tend to be associated with a true psychotic disorder and are less likely to be associated with stimulant use.

Methylphenidate (prescribed medications) and methamphetamine ("meth") are not the same substance.

There is no noticeable height difference in children who take stimulants compared to children who do not take stimulants.

Despite the many possible side effects of stimulants, one of the benefits of this class of medications is that your child can show improvements in focus and behaviors the first day you give the medication.

Strattera may be given at night and still work the next morning, but stimulants should not be given at bedtime to reduce the risk of worsened insomnia.

A Black Box Warning is the FDA's most stringent warning for drugs and medical devices on the market. Black Box warnings alert the public and health care providers to serious side effects, such as injury or death.

Both stimulants and Strattera have been associated with increases in suicidal thoughts and behaviors. However, only Strattera has a Black Box Warning for suicidal thinking even though the number of people with these findings was low.

In general, the benefits of treating ADHD outweigh the risks of the side effect profile of any medication.

Prescribing a medication "off-label" means that it does not have FDA approval to treat the disorder or symptom in question. "Off-label" prescribing does not speak to the appropriateness or effectiveness of the medication and it occurs frequently in medicine.

Except for ADHD, most mental illnesses have not been extensively studied in children. Therefore, most psychotropic medications and a few medications that treat ADHD in children are used "off-label" and are outside of FDA approval.

If no FDA-approved medication has helped your child with symptoms thought to be ADHD, consider having another assessment to confirm the diagnosis and rule out other coexisting diagnoses.

Bupropion (Wellbutrin) is not FDA-approved for treating depression in children under 18 years old or for treating ADHD.

Positive reinforcement: Giving a rewarding stimulus after a behavior.

Ex: Crystal gets candy (reward) when she eats all her dinner.

Negative reinforcement: Removing an aversive stimulus after a behavior.

Ex: Crystal can leave the dinner table (aversive stimulus) after she eats her dinner.

Extinction: The act of decreasing behavior by following it with an aversive stimulus.

Functional behavior analysis involves gathering information about the child's behaviors, what things cause them, and what happens after they end.

The ABC model is used to describe the events **A**ntecedent (before), the **B**ehavior itself, and the **C**onsequences of the behavior.

In the coercive process, parents and children respond negatively to each other until one gives in or "wins." This win reinforces the negative behaviors and makes both parties likely to repeat them and sometimes escalate them in the future to get the same result.

Behavioral interventions should certainly be attempted in all children with ADHD, but some factors seem to predict when a family will do better than others.

Medication appears to have greater impact on ADHD symptom reduction while behavioral intervention appears to have greater impact on some areas of functional impairment, including homework success and parenting.

No herbal treatment has been studied enough to prove that it is consistently effective in treating ADHD. Herbal treatments have side effects, some of which are very similar to those most parents want to avoid in stimulants. Herbal treatments have not been studied in large trials and have not been shown to be consistently effective for a majority of children.

CHAPTER FIVE

Treating Comorbid Disorders of ADHD

Several disorders commonly co-occur with ADHD and are called comorbid disorders. These can be other psychological, medical, or educational disorders. According to the CDC, about 64% of those with ADHD have a comorbid mental, emotional, or behavioral disorder.[32]

OPPOSITIONAL DEFIANT DISORDER

Oppositional defiant disorder (ODD) is the most commonly co-occurring disorder with ADHD. Specifically, 52% of children with ADHD have a behavior or conduct problem.[11]

ODD is a behavioral disorder in which children have problems with losing their temper, arguing with adults, deliberately annoying others and being easily annoyed themselves, blaming others for their mistakes or simply not taking responsibility for their wrongdoings, doing the opposite of what they are told or sometimes just not doing as they are told. He or she can be spiteful with their words and their actions and they can be extremely irritable and moody. Tantrums are a key feature of this disorder and they tend to occur when the child does not get his or her way, is told "no," or when something simple happens, like them not understanding an assignment. The primary caregiver is usually the one who is the recipient of the child with ODD's negative behaviors and moods. In most homes this is usually the mom or female authority figure. Dads tend to not see the behaviors, as the child is usually responsive to his requests. We are not sure why this is the case, but it is part of the reason that "I'm going to tell your daddy" works as effectively as it does. In mild cases, symptoms are predominantly seen only in the home. As severity worsens, symptoms can be directed at the non-primary caregiver and extend to places outside of the home, like school and church.

Like ADHD, ODD is diagnosed by clinical evaluation, but difficult cases may require psychological testing. Treatment of ODD may include therapy, medications, or a combination of both. In its Guide for Families regarding ODD, the American Academy of Child and Adolescent Psychiatry (AACAP) listed some therapeutic options for ODD: "Parent Management Training to help parents and others manage the child's behavior; Individual Psychotherapy to develop more effective anger management; Family Psychotherapy to improve communication and mutual understanding; Cognitive Problem-Solving Skills Training and Therapies to decrease negativity; and Social Skills Training to increase flexibility and improve social skills and frustration tolerance with peers."[33] Medications may help reduce symptoms of ODD that cause disturbances in the child's social, academic, and home lives, as well as the symptoms related to comorbid conditions such as ADHD, anxiety, and mood disorders.

CONDUCT DISORDER

Conduct disorder also falls under the 52% of children who have ADHD and a behavioral disorder.[11] According to the American Academy of Child and Adolescent Psychiatry (AACAP), conduct disorder "refers to a group of behavioral and emotional problems that are repetitive and persistent in children and adolescents. Children and adolescents with this disorder have great difficulty following rules, respecting the rights of others, showing empathy, and behaving in a socially acceptable way."[34] Often, children with conduct disorder are labeled as "bad" instead of mentally ill, and they are treated as such. Biological (brain damage), psychological (having a genetic makeup that may lend itself to conduct behaviors), and social factors (child neglect or abuse, school failure, traumatic life experiences) can lead to conduct disorder, though its cause is most likely multifactorial, like ADHD.

Diagnostically, children and adolescents with conduct disorder may exhibit some of the following behaviors: aggression or cruelty to people and animals, destruction of property, deceitfulness (including lying and stealing), and serious violation of rules.[34] Again, the diagnosis is a clinical one but psychological testing may be used in a difficult case. Treating conduct disorder is complex and can be very challenging. Many children will find themselves in trouble with the law, in need of social services like foster care, and/or abusing substances. Like ODD, treatment can also include behavior therapy and psychotherapy, medications for co-occurring ADHD and depression, and special education, when needed. AACAP also notes that there are some home-based treatment programs, such as Multisystemic Therapy (MST), that are "effective for helping both the child and the family."[34]

ANXIETY DISORDERS

Anxiety disorders commonly co-occur with ADHD. Up to 33% of children with ADHD also have anxiety.[7] Anxious children are often overly tense or uptight. Some may seek a lot of encouragement and their worries often interfere with activities.

Anxiety in children can have many different presentations including separation anxiety disorder, phobia, social anxiety disorder and fearing embarrassment or making a mistake, excessively worrying about family, school, or friends without any merited reason, and lacking self-confidence.

As with most other mental illnesses, treatment for anxiety disorders may include any of the following alone or in combination with each other: individual psychotherapy, family therapy, medications, behavioral treatments, and consultation with the school. Treating anxiety early on could mean that a child can better establish and maintain friendships, advance academically and professionally, and have a high self-esteem, all of which will propel the child toward success in and out of the classroom.

DEPRESSION

Seventeen percent (17%) of children with ADHD also have depression.[7] Even in children without ADHD, depression is not an uncommon finding in teenagers. Children and adults who are depressed often report or are noticed to feel or appear sad or irritable and/or tearful; have decreased interest in things that were enjoyable in the past; feel guilty about things that were not related to anything they did; have decreased energy; have poor concentration; have increases or decreases in appetite and/or weight and sleep; feel hopeless and/or worthless; and/or have thoughts of dying or wanting to kill himself or herself. Children who are depressed may also complain of physical ailments, like frequent headaches or stomach aches. Adolescents with depression may "self-medicate" with alcohol or other drugs as a way to remove the depression without having to admit to a professional that they are having depressive symptoms.

Regarding treatments, there are several effective treatments for depression. Therapy and medications are the two most common treatments for depression. Both cognitive behavioral therapy (CBT) and interpersonal therapy (IT) are evidence-based psychotherapies that have been found to be effective in the treatment of depression.[35] Especially when combined, psychotherapy and antidepressant medications can reduce depression. When to use antidepressants and which one to use should be determined on a case-by-case basis since some antidepressants can cause an increase in suicidal thoughts.[34] Despite this, the benefits of treating depression far outweigh the very small risk of medication-induced thoughts of self-harm as well as the risk of debilitation and decreased quality of life that can occur if depression is not treated at all.

AUTISM SPECTRUM DISORDER

Fourteen percent (14%) of children with ADHD also have autism spectrum disorder.[6] Autism spectrum disorder is a neurodevelopmental disorder. As its name suggests, it is one disorder with several presentations that fall on a spectrum. Autism is primarily a disorder of social skills and interactions but children with autism also have challenges with repetitive behaviors, speech development/delays, and nonverbal communication. Children with autism seem to exist in his or her own world, a place characterized by repetitive routines, odd and peculiar behaviors, problems in communication, and a total lack of social awareness or interest in others.[36] However, it is a spectrum and that means that no two children with autism will present the same.

Autism is characterized by deficits in social communication and social interaction as well as restricted, repetitive patterns of behaviors, interests, or activities. Children with autism can also be further classified as having or not having intellectual and speech deficits.

The symptoms of autism are usually identified and the diagnosis given by the time a child is 30 months old. It is often discovered when parents bring their child to medical attention with concerns about the child's speech, which could include an inability to talk or talk that seems unusual. Sometimes the child has stopped talking altogether. In other cases, the child has shown some changes in the way he or she socializes, like refusing to cuddle or avoiding interacting with others. Parents may also be concerned that their child cannot hear because he or she may not respond when his or her name is called.

Some of the early signs and symptoms that suggest a young child may need further evaluation for autism include:[36]

- no smiling by six months old
- no back and forth sharing of sounds, smiles, or facial expressions by nine months old
- not responding when their name is called
- no babbling, pointing, reaching, or waving by 12 months

- no single words by 16 months
- no two-word phrases by 24 months
- regression in development at any age
- any loss of speech, babbling, or social skills

A preschool age child with "classic" autism is generally withdrawn, indifferent, and fails to respond to other people. Many children with autism do not make eye contact. They may also engage in odd or ritualistic behaviors like rocking, hand flapping, or an obsessive need to maintain order.

Many children with autism do not speak at all while others speak in a rhyming pattern. Still, others have echolalia, which means they repeat phrases like an echo, or they refer to themselves in third person by using pronouns such as "he" or "she."

The severity of autism varies from mild to severe and all in between. Some children are very bright and excel academically while still having problems with social and peer interactions. These children may be able to live very typical lives in adulthood, including living independently. (You may hear non-medical professionals refer to children in this category as "high functioning.") Other children with autism may have an intellectual disability and may need help with activities of daily living in childhood and adulthood. (Note that of all children with autism, 31% have an intellectual disability (intelligence quotient [IQ] < 70), 25% are in the borderline range (IQ 71–85), and 44% have IQ scores in the average to above average range (i.e., IQ > 85).[37] Occasionally, a child with autism may seem gifted or what some call a "natural talent" in art or music, for example, but this is not always the case, though actors often portray it in movies this way.

There is no known cause of autism, but it is known that vaccinations do not cause autism. Neither is there a treatment for autism spectrum disorder, specifically, but ADHD and behavioral and aggressive symptoms may be treated with medication. Applied behavioral analysis (ABA), a specific type of behavioral therapy, has also been shown to be helpful for some children.

TOURETTE SYNDROME

Tourette syndrome occurs in about 1% of children with ADHD.[7] Tourette syndrome is a disorder that involves uncontrollable, sudden, brief, unwanted repetitive movements and sounds (tics). This diagnosis requires that multiple motor tics and at least one vocal tic be present for one year.[38] Some common tics are shoulder shrugging, eye blinking, grunting, head jerking, coughing, and throat clearing. In extreme cases the tics can be painful. There is no cure for Tourette's but there are some treatments available that can decrease pain, make the tics more tolerable, and improve the patient's quality of life.

SLEEP DISORDERS

It is estimated that 25-50% of people with ADHD experience sleep problems that range from insomnia to secondary sleep conditions.[39] Children with ADHD can have problems falling asleep, staying asleep, and/or waking up. They can also have problems with sleep-disordered breathing, obstructive sleep apnea, and restless leg syndrome. Adequately treating children's and adolescents' insomnia is key to their overall performance inside and out of the classroom.

Children and adolescents should also have good bedtime hygiene. This should include the same few activities that give a signal to the body that it is time to leave the daytime activities and go to those that involve sleeping. Taking a warm bath and reading a calming book are some activities that can be included in sleep hygiene. One would not want to exercise, listen to loud, heavy music before bed, or even look at cell phones, gaming systems, or the TV just before or while in bed.

Regarding sleep, I was quoted as saying, "In general, the impact of ADHD on sleep changes as the child ages. Younger children with ADHD tend to be more hyperactive, and therefore are more likely to move about and show signs of restlessness as they attempt to fall asleep. Adolescents with ADHD tend to have less hyperactive symptoms during the day but still have problems staying asleep through the night. Because of their age, adolescents can stay awake longer; however, later bedtimes may complicate the picture of a child who has trouble falling asleep. Developmentally, adolescents often brag about needing less sleep than younger children, but a full night's rest is still important for them."[40]

LEARNING DISORDERS

Children with ADHD often have co-occurring learning disorders. These can include dyslexia (difficulty with reading), dyscalculia (difficulty with math), or dysgraphia (difficulty with writing). Children with these and other learning disorders may need extra, specialized help from their school, including special education services.[41] (See Chapter 6: "Advocating for Your Child with ADHD.")

DIFFICULT PEER RELATIONSHIPS

Some children with ADHD have trouble establishing and maintaining friendships. Children with inattentive symptoms may seem shy or withdrawn to their peers. Children who are impulsive and/or hyperactive may be rejected by their peers because they are intrusive, may not wait their turn, and/or may act aggressively.

RISK FOR INJURY

According to the CDC, "children and adolescents with ADHD are likely to get hurt more often and more severely than peers without ADHD. Research indicates that children with ADHD are significantly more likely to get injured while walking or riding a bicycle, have head injuries, injure more than one part of their body, be hospitalized for unintentional poisoning, have near-drowning or drowning experiences, be admitted to intensive care units, or have an injury resulting in disability."[41]

The most likely reason children with ADHD get injured is because of their inattention and impulsive behaviors. For example, a young child might forget to look both ways before running in the street to retrieve a wandering ball. A teenager may impulsively ingest, smoke, or drink something dangerous offered to them. Or an older teenager may speed while driving, change lanes without looking, or disregard a traffic signal while driving.

PARENTAL MENTAL ILLNESS

While it is important for your child with ADHD to be treated for any comorbid mental health disorders, your mental illnesses (as the parent) must be treated as well. As was mentioned earlier, 51% of fathers and 41% of mothers of children with ADHD have ADHD themselves and pass it to their children.[4] This means that it is highly likely that one of your child's parents (you or the other parent!) has ADHD, too. Unfortunately, most parents' ADHD has never been diagnosed or their ADHD is not treated in adulthood. If this identifies you, you may notice that you are less likely to be patient and are more likely to be irritable and short-tempered with your children. Independent of a primary mental illness, parents can have a secondary depression that results from having children with mental illnesses. Recall that children with ADHD can be hyperactive and even irritable, and this sometimes means that obtaining childcare can be difficult. This can then lead to parents being isolated from their friends and a strain on marital relationships, which can lead to depression. Parents of children with ADHD can also experience anxiety. They worry if their child's school will call and they will have to leave their jobs. They worry if their child will be injured because of their impulsivity. And they worry that their local child welfare agency will become involved after their child is hurt due to their impulsivity.

SPOTLIGHT

It has been proven that vaccines DO NOT cause autism.

Parents, it is imperative that you take care of your own mental health so you are better prepared to handle the stressors and challenges that may come with managing your child's mental illness.

CHAPTER SIX

Advocating for Your Child with ADHD

Children with ADHD have the potential to do very well academically and socially, and to be successful in the classroom and in life. However, they may need extra help academically and the educational support services to do so. This is where your role as an advocate may become important. While your child's school may recognize the need for extra help and then begin the process to put it in place on their own, they may not and you may have to advocate for your child to receive it. Likewise, you may have to advocate for your child to receive a thorough medical and psychological evaluation to rule out any medical look-alikes that could confound an ADHD diagnosis. Lastly, you must advocate for others in your family, including your spouse/significant other and children, to ensure their emotional needs are being met.

SPECIAL EDUCATION

Special education exists to provide the personalized education your child may need. Many parents shy away from special education services or sometimes even refuse them because they do not want the negative connotation associated with those services. Parents often recall receiving "LD" (for learning disability or disabled) services themselves when they were in school and the lowered self-esteem and even the bullying they experienced while in those classes. They may also recall being isolated in what are now called self-contained classrooms and not being in class with their peers who were in general education, and do not understand that the current goal is to include students in classes with their peers when possible.

Federal law has required public schools to provide services for children who learn differently from others for almost 40 years. These services, called special education, should be available to any child with a learning disability who is from 3 years old to 21 years old and who is also eligible to receive them. (Note that not all children with learning disabilities will qualify for special education services.) The Individuals with Disabilities Education Act, or IDEA, was originally named in 1990 and "exists to ensure all children with special education needs obtain them and that the rights of children with disabilities and their parents are protected."[42] The most current name of the law today is the Individuals with Disabilities Education Improvement Act of 2004 (IDEIA 2004), but it is simplified again to IDEA, which is the more commonly known version of the law. Both state and federal laws require schools' teachers and administrators to work with parents to create individualized education programs, which are road maps that guide a student's individualized learning. This means that children with disabilities have a right to special education and that schools are not simply giving in to parents' requests, nor doing the child a favor.[42]

Part of the rights of children with disabilities is that they have a legal right to free appropriate public education (FAPE). FAPE services should meet the child's unique needs, which means they will differ from one child to another, and should allow the child to benefit educationally. These services are outlined annually in the child's Individualized Education Plan (IEP).

Part of meeting IDEA's FAPE is that the child must have the opportunity to interact with other children his or her age as often as possible, which means that your child must be educated in the least restrictive environment (LRE). Under the LRE, two things should happen a) your child will spend all day in a typical classroom and receive the appropriate services and supports designed to enable him or her to participate successfully, and b) your child will be removed from that setting only when his or her Individualized Education Plan (IEP) cannot be successfully implemented there.

To help parents navigate the special education system, there exists the Protection and Advocacy Systems (P&As).

These federally funded agencies are in every state and they help parents navigate the very complex special education system by providing legal advocacy services to help you protect your child's education rights.

ADVOCATE FOR SPECIAL EDUCATION: THE INDIVIDUALIZED EDUCATION PLAN (IEP)

Your child's school may present the idea of an Individualized Education Plan (IEP) or a 504 Plan. However, if they do not, you need to be prepared to advocate for your child so that he or she may get the special education services to which they are entitled.

To be eligible for special education and related services under the IDEA, a child must first be identified as a "child with a disability." To have this identification, a child must meet federal and state eligibility criteria for at least one of the following thirteen disability categories: "autism, deaf-blindness, developmental delay (young children ages 3-9), emotional disability (formerly emotional disturbance), hearing impairment (including deafness); intellectual disability (formerly mental retardation); multiple disabilities, orthopedic impairment; other health impairment, specific learning disability, speech or language impairment, traumatic brain injury, visual impairment (including blindness)."[42]

A child must have a special education evaluation at the expense of the school district to determine if he or she meets one of the thirteen named disability categories. This evaluation determines if your child has a disability as defined under the IDEA and if he or she will be eligible for special education and related services. This evaluation will also identify the type and amount of services your child will need.

You may refer your child for an evaluation. The request does not need to be in writing but it is a good idea for parents to write a letter as a means of recordkeeping. You should include some key components in the letter, including the

- Date: Recall the IEP has a specific timeline so you want to know when it starts.

- Addressee: Address the letter to the leader of the Special Education Department

- Introduction: Let the addressee know who you are and how you are related to the child. (EX: "I am Mrs. Barbara Jackson, Bobby Jackson's mother.")

- Explanation of the Problem(s): Let the addressee know your concerns. (EX: "John is having problems in reading," or "Mary is having problems in math" are two examples. You may also add something like "He cannot stay in his seat" or "She talks all the time and misses your instructions.")

- Request: State what you want. (EX: "I want him/her to be evaluated to see if he/she qualifies for special education or other extra help in school.")

- Acknowledge time guidelines: Make the school aware of your understanding that time guidelines exist. (EX: "I understand that this is time-sensitive and we have a specific amount of time to complete this evaluation.)

- State your desire to participate: Let the team know that you are aware that you have to participate in the process. (EX: "Please let me know when the evaluation team will meet so I can attend and sign the paperwork for the initial evaluation.")

- Your contact information: Let them know how they can reach you. (EX: "You can contact me at (123) 456-7890 or at email@address.com.")

- Closing: Set expectations for the future. (EX: "Thank you for reading my letter. I look forward to hearing from you soon about next steps.")

- Closing and signature: Use something like "sincerely" to close the letter. Sign it if it is handwritten.

- Carbon copy (CC): CC others who may need to be involved, like the principal and/or superintendent. Include their name(s) and title(s). Make sure you send a copy to their email address(es) or hand deliver a copy to them, depending on your choice for delivery.

Lastly, make sure you keep an electronic or handwritten copy for yourself.

After the evaluation referral (request) is made by either the school or the parent, an IEP Team, which includes the parents, will meet to decide if the child should be evaluated. This meeting should take place in a timely manner, though the IDEA does not give a specific time frame for the meeting to occur. (Some school districts meet as early as 15 days after receiving the referral.) One of two decisions will come from this meeting:

- The IEP Team refuses to evaluate the child. In this case the IEP Team must provide a written explanation of why and how this decision was made. Your child should also be considered for eligibility under Section 504 or referred to the school's Problem-Solving Team, a process that may be called Response to Intervention (RTI). Parents may challenge the IEP Team's decision using the conflict resolution mechanisms that the IDEA provides.

- The IEP Team determines that the child needs further evaluation for special education services. In this case, the parent must give written consent for evaluation. Consent can be given at the IEP Team meeting and the timeline to complete the evaluation process begins at that time.

DAY 1	BY DAY 60	BY DAY 90	BY DAY 120
Parent signs paperwork for testing/evaluation.	All evaluations must be completed.	The IEP Team must meet to determine the child's eligibility.	The IEP must be written and then implemented as soon as possible afterwards.

If your referral for evaluation of your child was denied, your child may be considered for a 504 or to work with the school's Problem-Solving Team (PST), which could also be called Response to Intervention (RTI). States may vary on laws and practices concerning the PST/RTI. For example, some states may require PST/RTI for up to eight weeks before a child is evaluated for special education eligibility. There are cases that are exceptions and these allow for the RTI requirement to be waived. Children who may be eligible for a waiver include those who have severe problems that require immediate attention and include those who are three, four, or five years old who have not been in kindergarten; have only articulation, voice, or fluency problems; have a medical diagnosis of traumatic brain injury; or have been referred by a parent for evaluation.[43] Most states do not have this law, although they may have this as a common practice.

Once your child has an IEP, he or she should be reevaluated at least once every three years, per IDEA. An annual IEP meeting should be held each year to make sure your child's academic needs are still being met by the plan.

ADVOCATE FOR SPECIAL EDUCATION: SECTION 504

Section 504 of the Rehabilitation Act of 1973 (Section 504) ensures school children with disabilities receive the services they need. This is how it is similar to IDEA. On the other hand, Section 504 is a civil rights statute. (A civil rights statute bans any program that receives federal funds from discriminating against potential participants. Schools receive federal dollars and persons with disabilities can be victims of discrimination by not receiving services they need in school. These are reasons for Section 504.)[42] Section 504 is also unlike IDEA because Section 504 gives less directives to schools about how, when, or who is involved in the process of giving students the services they need. This means that you as the parent will need to make sure that the process moves in a timely and efficient manner and that you are involved in each step of the process so that you can remain informed of each step of the process.

Recall that IDEA only applies to children who have one of thirteen physical, mental, emotional, or sensory impairments that are recognized disability categories under the IDEA, *and* who have been found to need special education and related services. A Section 504 (commonly called "a 504") may be the next best thing for your child if they do not qualify for an IEP.

To be eligible under Section 504, a child must either be permanently or temporarily mentally or physically impaired; have had an impairment in the past; or must be thought to be impaired. Section 504 regulations do not give a list of diagnoses or disorders that qualify for services, unlike in IDEA. They do, however, provide this description: "a physical or mental impairment is any physiological disorder or condition, cosmetic disfigurement, or anatomical loss affecting one or more body systems, such as neurological, musculoskeletal, special sense organs, respiratory (including speech organs), cardiovascular, reproductive, digestive, genitourinary, immune, circulatory, hemic, lymphatic, skin, and endocrine; or any mental or psychological disorder, such as an intellectual disability [formerly mental retardation], organic brain syndrome, emotional or mental illness, and specific learning disabilities."[42]

Section 504 requires that one major life activity be affected by your child's disability to be considered an impairment. Examples of major life activities and major bodily functions that can be affected include such things as "caring for oneself, performing manual tasks, seeing, hearing, eating, sleeping, walking, standing, sitting, speaking, breathing, learning, reading, concentrating, thinking, communicating, interacting with others, and working, and the operation of a major bodily function, including those of the immune, digestive, genitourinary, neurological, brain, respiratory, and circulatory systems, among others, are also considered major life activities."[42] This list is not exhaustive, so an activity or function that is not listed here may still be a major life activity. Disabilities or conditions that are not constant and only occur in episodes can qualify for Section 504 as long as they impair a major life activity when they are active. For example, epilepsy and asthma, both of which do not occur on a consistent basis, can impair life activities and, therefore, would qualify for Section 504.

ADVOCATE FOR SPECIAL EDUCATION: THE CHILD WHO ATTENDS PRIVATE SCHOOL

If a child attends private school, he or she may or may not be eligible for special education services. Specifically, IDEA states that a private school does not have to provide the same special education services to a child as he or she would receive in a public school. IDEA states that local public school districts must do the following things for students in private school: "evaluate the student for special education if a referral has been made; determine if a student is eligible for special education; develop an appropriate Instructional School Plan (ISP) for the child's school; and consult with parents and the student's teachers when developing an Instructional School Plan."[44] Once the special education evaluation is completed and the ISP is written, the public school administrators decide what services they will provide. It is important to know that the above information is only true when parents elect to place their child in a private school. If the public school recommended a private school for the child, the public school district has to make sure that the student gets all services that are legally due him or her.

ADVOCATE FOR THOROUGH MEDICAL AND PSYCHIATRIC EVALUATION

Sometimes, appropriately, parents have a "gut feeling" that something else may be happening with their child. And in certain instances, they may be correct. Here are some common ADHD look-alikes:

- General: The child may be demonstrating age-appropriate behavior and the parents only need education about typical child development.

- Classroom related: The child may perform above or below what is expected for their grade level and this can lead to the child appearing "bored" or behaving inappropriately in the classroom. An IEP may still be warranted in these cases.

- Medical: Absence seizures, sleep disorders, constipation, and vision problems are common medical problems that have been confused for ADHD. Medical treatment is recommended in each of these instances.

- Psychiatric: Bipolar, anxiety, and depressive disorders can all have symptoms that can be confused with ADHD.

ADVOCATE FOR THE CHILD'S FAMILY AND SUPPORT SYSTEM

Any child with a special need will require special amounts of time, energy, effort, and money. It is important that parents make time to attend to the emotional and academic needs of others in the home, including themselves and their adult partners.

SPOTLIGHT

Think of SPECIAL education as UNIQUE education to help reduce the negative connotation associated with the phrase.

Having a diagnosis does not mean a child will be eligible for special education services. The symptoms of the diagnosis must cause impairment that adversely affects the child's educational performance.

Attention deficit hyperactivity disorder (ADHD) is one of the chronic health problems listed as an example of "other health impairment."

If you disagree with your school district's evaluation of your child, you can request for an outside agency to evaluate your child at the school district's expense. This is called an Independent Educational Evaluation (IEE).[42]

The school has 120 calendar days, not school days, to complete the evaluation process from the time you sign the consent forms for evaluation.

The timeline for testing does not begin until the parent signs the consent for it to happen, so this must be done right away!

Even if you do not consent for your child to be tested, the IDEA has mediation and due process procedures to allow the school to pursue an evaluation of the child if the child attends public school.

There is a lot of variability between states regarding whether a child is required to participate in Response to Intervention (RTI) before being evaluated for special education eligibility. Review your state's rules for clarification.

Response to Intervention (RTI) is a multi-tier approach to the early identification and support of students with specialized and individualized learning and behavior needs. The RTI process begins with high-quality instruction and universal screening of all children in the general education classroom.[44]

CHAPTER SEVEN

Moving Forward with ADHD

Now that you know more than the basics about ADHD, what's next? It's simple! Help your child obtain SUCCESS!

S **Say the diagnosis.** Be honest with yourself about your child's diagnosis. Know that you cannot heal what you won't reveal. Accepting the diagnosis is the first best thing you can do to help your child and yourself. Learn all you can about the diagnosis and use your learnings to advocate for your child. As appropriate for their age, empower your child to demand the special things they need to learn and develop but *challenge them to reach for the stars and to shine as if they know they already are one.*

U **Utilize your child's teacher and seek special education services.** Know that teachers are you and your child's friends. During the school year, teachers likely spend more hours with your child when he or she is awake than you do. They know the specifics of what it takes for your child to thrive academically. *Worry very little about your child being labeled, for teachers likely have already recognized how your child behaves and learns differently from the other students, and labels only help us know how to best help your child.*

C **Composure: Keep yours.** Living with ADHD is hard! The children are stressed, confused, and frustrated because they WANT to behave and perform better but they do not know how or why they do not. Their poor behaviors, academic disappointments, and irritability can infuriate the best parent and can cause them to lose their cool. Remember, *be patient with your child, for ADHD is not a choice, and you can work to prevent it from being a devastating challenge.*

C **Correct the symptoms with treatment.** Psychostimulant medications are the most consistent at effectively treating ADHD. Your child needs to attend, plan, be calm, and make informed decisions every day, so you should strongly consider giving medications every day. (Young children are likely to hurt themselves by jumping off furniture at home after school hours. Adolescents are likely to use drugs and alcohol after school hours. And adolescents are most likely to engage in motor vehicle accidents and moving traffic violations after school hours.) Behavioral modification plays a very important role in treatment and should be combined with medications. Supplemental treatments have not been proven to be consistently effective and have no associated large-scale studies to prove their safety or effectiveness. Remember, *adequately treat your child's ADHD now, or he or she may self-medicate themselves in the future.*

E **Exemplify organization and consistency.** All children need consistency, but children with ADHD perform and behave best when there is consistency and organization. *Children with untreated ADHD have behaviors that are inconsistently inconsistent, so surrounding them with organization and consistency at least places some routine in their lives.*

S **Stay positive.** Release yourself from the guilt associated with having a child with ADHD and for treating them. Encourage your child to move toward their goals with their head high. Prepare for the day when the challenges that worry you now will be memories of the past. Resist negativity from others. When others question you by saying you are only giving your child a crutch, *remind them that a crutch has its place if a leg is broken and that one day the leg, and your baby, will heal!*

S **SHINE.** Make and repeat your affirmations and six-word mantras (ex: "My child will get better soon!").

Keep the faith! Stay the course! Know that *ADHD may be a DISability, but with the proper treatment your child can claim SUCCESS and can brag "I have THIS ABILITY!!!"* With you by their side, your child will SHINE!

THANK YOU

Thank you to the moms and dads of children with ADHD. Thank you for being strong and courageous, and for tackling parenthood of a differently abled child with the grace you do. Thank you for loving your children even when frustrated. And thank you for continuing to seek education so that you can parent them the best way they need it. Thank you to every one of my patients. Many years into my career, I still learn and will continue to learn from you. May you all be blessed with many years of happiness, peace, calmness, and success, in and out of the classroom.

NOTES

1. "ADHD and Brain Structure and Function," Healthline, Accessed October 8, 2020, https://www.healthline.com/health/adhd/the-brains-structure-and-function.

2. Kimberly Holland and Elsbeth Riley, "ADHD Numbers: Facts, Statistics, and You," The A.D.D. Resource Center, October 11, 2017, https://www.addrc.org/adhd-numbers-facts-statistics-and-you.

3. Psych Central, "The Genetics of ADHD," Accessed January 2, 2021. https://psychcentral.com/lib/the-genetics-of-adhd#1.

4. Medical News Today, "Is ADHD Genetic? Everything You Need to Know," Accessed January 2, 2021, https://www.medicalnewstoday.com/articles/325594.

5. Carolyn Todd, "Why Are So Many More Children Being Diagnosed with ADHD Today?," Self, September 24, 2018, https://www.self.com/story/adhd-diagnosis-rates-children-increase.

6. Candy Gulko, "Focus on Epilepsy: Epilepsy and ADHD: A Bidirectional Relationship," MedPage Today, October 11,

2018, https://www.medpagetoday.com/resource-centers/focus-on-epilepsy/epilepsy-and-adhd-bidirectional-relationship/2235.

7. Centers for Disease Control and Prevention, "Attention-Deficit/Hyperactivity Disorder (ADHD): Data and Statistics," November 16, 2020, https://www.cdc.gov/ncbddd/adhd/data.html.

8. Rachel Bluth, "ADHD numbers are rising, and scientists are trying to understand why," *The Washington Post*, September 12, 2018, https://www.washingtonpost.com/national/health-science/adhd-numbers-are-rising-and-scientists-are-trying-to-understand-why/2018/09/07/a918d0f4-b07e-11e8-a20b-5f4f84429666_story.html.

9. Joel Nigg, PhD, "ADHD Clinicians Must Consider Racial Bias in Evaluation and Treatment of Black Children," Accessed October 8, 2020, https://www.additudemag.com/racial-bias-impairs-adhd-diagnosis-treatment/.

10. Children and Adults with Attention-Deficit/Hyperactivity Disorder (CHADD), "General Prevalence of ADHD," Accessed January 2, 2021, https://chadd.org/about-adhd/general-prevalence.

11. Healthline Parenthood, "Gender Differences in ADHD Symptoms," Accessed January 2, 2021, https://www.healthline.com/health/adhd/adhd-symptoms-in-girls-and-boys.

12. William D. Smucker, MD, and Marjaneh Hedayat, MD, "Evaluation and Treatment of ADHD," *American Family Physician*, September 1, 2001, 64(5):817-830, https://www.aafp.org/afp/2001/0901/p817.html.

13. Michelle Shepard, MD, PhD, and David Rettew, MD, "Diagnostic Tools for the Initial Evaluation of ADHD and Monitoring Treatment Success," Accessed October 10, 2020, http://contentmanager.med.uvm.edu/docs/diagnostic_tools_for_the_initial_evaluation_of_adhd_and_monitoring_treatment_success/vchip-documents/diagnostic_tools_for_the_initial_evaluation_of_adhd_and_monitoring_treatment_success.pdf?sfvrsn=3ca1774b_2.

14. Staff Writers, "Nurse Practitioner vs Doctor (Physician)," Nurse Practitioner Schools, October 26, 2020, https://www.nursepractitionerschools.com/faq/np-vs-doctor/.

15. "Psychological vs. Neuropsychological Testing," Neuro Assessment & Development Center Psychological & Neuropsychological Testing, Accessed October 10, 2020, https://www.neurodevelop.com/PsychvsNpsych.

16. Dr. David Velkoff, "T.O.V.A: An Accurate Assessment for Attention Deficit Disorders?," Drake Institute of Neurophysical Medicine, Accessed January 10, 2021, https://www.drakeinstitute.com/tova-testing-for-add-and-adhd.

17. Rachel G. Klein, PhD, et al., "Clinical and Functional Outcome of Childhood ADHD 33 Years Later," Archives of General Psychiatry, December 1, 2012, 69(12):1295-1303, https://doi.org/10.1001/archgenpsychiatry.2012.271.

18. "Attention Deficit Hyperactivity Disorder in Adults," WedMD, Accessed January 10, 2021, https://www.webmd.com/add-adhd/adhd-adults.

19. "ADHD Parents Medication Guide," American Academy of Child and Adolescent Psychiatry and Child and American Psychiatric Association, accessed January 19, 2021, https://www.aacap.org/App_Themes/AACAP/docs/resource_centers/resources/med_guides/adhd_parents_medication_guide_english.pdf.

20. Andrew Adesman, "The ADHD Medication Guide ©," Cohen Children's Medical Center, Accessed January 10, 2021, http://www.adhdmedicationguide.com/.

21. "ADHD: Primary Care Perspectives," UTMB, Accessed January 10, 2021, https://www.utmb.edu/pedi_ed/GENPEDS/ADHD/page_16.htm.

22. S A Hemmer, J F Pasternak, S G Zecker, B L Trommer, "Stimulant Therapy and Seizure Risk in Children with ADHD," February 2001, 24(2):99-102, doi: 10.1016/s0887-8994(00)00240-x.

23. "Autism Spectrum Disorder Fact Sheet," National Institute of Neurological Disorders and Stroke, Accessed December 20, 2020, https://www.ninds.nih.gov/disorders/patient-caregiver-education/fact-sheets/autism-spectrum-disorder-fact-sheet.

24. Michael Craig Miller, MD, "Commentary: ADHD Drugs and Heart Risk for Children," Harvard Health Publishing, February 2012, https://www.health.harvard.edu/newsletter_article/adhd-drugs-and-heart-risk-for-children.

25. "Could Your Child's Meds Affect His Height? Likely Not," CHADD, ADHD Weekly, May 23, 2019, https://chadd.org/adhd-weekly/could-your-childs-meds-affect-his-height-likely-not/.

26. "Non-Stimulant Medications Available for ADHD Treatment," American Academy of Pediatrics, June 17, 2016, https://www.healthychildren.org/English/health-issues/conditions/adhd/Pages/Non-Stimulant-Medications-Available-for-ADHD-Treatment.aspx.

27. Linda Pfiffner, Lauren Haack, "Behavior Management for School Aged Children with ADHD," Child Adolescent Psychiatry Clinical N Am, October 2014, 23(4): 731-746, doi: 10.1016/j.chc.2014.05.014.

28. "Study Shows Omega-3s Benefit Some Children with ADHD," CHADD, ADHD Weekly, January 16, 2020,

https://chadd.org/adhd-weekly/study-shows-omega-3s-benefit-some-children-with-adhd/.

29. "Fish and Omega-3 Fatty Acids," American Heart Association, March 23, 2017, https://www.heart.org/en/healthy-living/healthy-eating/eat-smart/fats/fish-and-omega-3-fatty-acids.

30. "Are There Natural Remedies for ADHD?," Medical News Today, Accessed January 18, 2021, https://www.medicalnewstoday.com/articles/315239.

31. "Neurofeedback (EEG Biofeedback)," CHADD, Accessed January 10, 2021, https://chadd.org/about-adhd/neurofeedback-eeg-biofeedback/.

32. "Attention-Deficit/Hyperactivity Disorder (ADHD)," Medical Home Portal, Accessed January 18, 2021, https://www.medicalhomeportal.org/diagnoses-and-conditions/attention-deficit-hyperactivity-disorder.

33. "ODD: A Guide for Families," American Academy of Child and Adolescent Psychiatry, 2009, https://www.aacap.org/App_Themes/AACAP/docs/resource_centers/odd/odd_resource_center_odd_guide.pdf.

34. "Conduct Disorder," Facts for Families, American Academy of Child and Adolescent Psychiatry, June 2018, No. 33, https://www.aacap.org/AACAP/Families_and_Youth/

Facts_for_Families/FFF-Guide/Conduct-Disorder-033.aspx.

35. "Depression Treatment and Management," Anxiety and Depression Association of America, Accessed January 18, 2021, https://adaa.org/understanding-anxiety/depression-treatment-management.

36. "Autism Spectrum Disorders," Facts for Families, American Academy of Child and Adolescent Psychiatry, June 2018, No. 11, https://www.aacap.org/AACAP/Families_and_Youth/Facts_for_Families/FFF-Guide/The-Child-With-Autism-011.aspx.

37. "Autism Statistics and Facts," Autism Speaks, Accessed January 18, 2021, https://www.autismspeaks.org/autism-statistics.

38. American Psychiatric Association, (2013), *Diagnostic and Statistical Manual Of Mental Disorders* (5th ed.), Arlington, VA.

39. "ADHD and Sleep," SleepFoundation.org, January 15, 2021, https://www.sleepfoundation.org/mental-health/adhd-and-sleep.

40. Dr. Brandi Bolling, "Sleep and ADHD," The Mattress Nerd, November 2, 2020, https://www.mattressnerd.com/sleep-and-adhd/.

41. "Other Concerns and Conditions with ADHD," Center for Disease Control and Prevention, September 4, 2020, https://www.cdc.gov/ncbddd/adhd/conditions.html.

42. Special Education in Alabama: A Right Not a Favor, Alabama Disabilities Advocacy Program, July 2014, https://adap.ua.edu/uploads/5/7/8/9/57892141/rnfcomplete_book.pdf.

43. "Learn About RTI," RTI Action Network, Accessed December 10, 2020, http://www.rtinetwork.org/learn.

44. "Private School and Special Education Services," UnderstandingSpecialEducation.com, Accessed January 20, 2021, https://www.understandingspecialeducation.com/private-school.html.

ABOUT THE AUTHOR

Dr. Brandi J. Rudolph Bolling is a triple-board-certified adult psychiatrist, child and adolescent psychiatrist, and pediatrician. Although attention deficit hyperactivity disorder (ADHD) and autism spectrum disorders are her specialties, she carries extensive knowledge about many mental health topics. Practicing for nearly ten years, she has seen approximately 20,000 patients. Through her concierge practice and speaking engagements, she helps mothers of and educators who teach children with ADHD gain the education they need so they can help their children and students be empowered, be engaged, be encouraged, and be successful in the classroom and in life.

Dr. Brandi B obtained her bachelor of science in neuroscience from Vanderbilt University and her medical degree (MD) from Meharry Medical College. She completed her triple board residency program at Indiana University School of Medicine. She works in a variety of medical settings for children and adults in rural and urban areas alike, and she offers her patients a cutting-edge approach to their mental health care regimen.

Dr. Brandi B takes pride in increasing awareness of the importance of caring for one's mental health through media, social media, small group, and conference settings. She frequently serves on medical and mental health panels and as a keynote speaker in both face-to-face and virtual settings. She also hosts an annual summit, which teaches parents, educators, and medical professionals about ADHD. She hosts a weekly livestream, "Focus on It Friday," every Friday at noon (CST) on her Facebook page, Dr. BrandiB.

Follow Dr. Brandi B on Facebook and all social media @DrBrandiB or @DrBrandi_B

CREATING DISTINCTIVE BOOKS
WITH INTENTIONAL RESULTS

We're a collaborative group of creative masterminds with a mission to produce high-quality books to position you for monumental success in the marketplace.

Our professional team of writers, editors, designers, and marketing strategists work closely together to ensure that every detail of your book is a clear representation of the message in your writing.

Want to know more?
Write to us at info@publishyourgift.com
or call (888) 949-6228

Discover great books, exclusive offers, and more at
www.PublishYourGift.com

Connect with us on social media

@publishyourgift

www.ingramcontent.com/pod-product-compliance
Ingram Content Group UK Ltd.
Pitfield, Milton Keynes, MK11 3LW, UK
UKHW022209230426
12048UKWH00016BA/743